Linear Programming and
Cash Management/CASH ALPHA

Linear Programming and Cash Management/CASH ALPHA

Robert F. Calman

The M. I. T. Press
Massachusetts Institute of Technology
Cambridge, Massachusetts, and London, England

Library of Congress catalog card number: 68-18233

FOREWORD

Every year the faculty of the Alfred P. Sloan School of Management of Massachusetts Institute of Technology awards the Brooks Prize to the best Master's thesis submitted by a student during the year. The Prize is named after E. P. Brooks, the first Dean of the School. From the time the prize was first awarded, the winning theses have reflected a remarkably high quality of analytical research. They fully reflect the faculty's conviction that modern analytic approaches to management are not mere academic curiosities but possess immediate applications to a fascinating range of practical problems.

Robert F. Calman, winner of the Brooks Prize in 1967, after receiving a Sloan Fellowship in Executive Development, continues in this short but rich tradition. With a clarity that belies its complex underpinnings, Calman's thesis describes the application of quantitative methods to an important financial problem in a manner that makes it available to executives who have no special mathematical skills. It is not only good research but good pedagogy as well. This monograph, adapted by Mr. Calman from his thesis, should not only aid corporate industrial managers in managing their deposits but should also speed the rapid, adaptive responses taking place in bank management.

Paul H. Cootner
Professor of Finance

Alfred P. Sloan School of Management
Massachusetts Institute of Technology

PREFACE

This book describes how I feel a major company should evaluate its
banking relationships, individually and as a *system*, and then suggests how
it can utilize linear programming to aid in making optimum decisions on the
placement of discretionary banking business, based on short-run (monthly)
forecasts of activity, and also to test possible structural changes of the system.
It was written, while I was an Alfred P. Sloan Fellow at M.I.T., in partial
fulfillment of the requirements for the degree of Master of Science.
  "CASH ALPHA" is simply the name I have given to the linear programming
model of a firm's banking system developed in this study and, more generally,
to the over-all approach I have used of treating a firm's banking relationships
as a systems problem.
  CASH ALPHA owes a great deal to the operations researchers' concentration
on inventory management problems in recent years. Many of the problems
facing the financial manager in the design of a cash collection system are
similar to the problems facing production and sales management in inventory
control. For example, the selection of lock-box banks for the collection of
receivables is very much like the warehouse siting problem.
  CASH ALPHA also owes much to the cost-of-capital concept, which provides
an economic drive for divestment of redundant assets, wherever they may be.
CASH ALPHA, in its broader definition, is also in debt to the often-heard
pronouncement that if banks are not compensated adequately through the

medium of compensating balances for the myriad services they provide, they will have to charge cash fees for such services. As will be shown, this is not necessarily an unappealing idea from the bank customer's standpoint.

CASH ALPHA represents a philosophy that is peculiarly my own. My experience as a financial officer in industry and as a bank loan officer is a major determinant of this philosophy, but CASH ALPHA is not a reflection of any one experience or any one institution. I am the major "input" into the design of CASH ALPHA; but if I am CASH ALPHA's "architect," Paul S. Nix of Mobil Oil Corporation's Operations Research Department is its "master builder," helping me to write some equations, supplying those equations that eluded me, and helping me to understand the significance of the computer's seemingly endless outpouring of data. Also, I am indebted to several "sidewalk superintendents" — friends at several banks around the country who invested their time to understand CASH ALPHA, and then freely gave some excellent "feedback" that I have integrated into the model. I am indebted to Dr. Paul H. Cootner, Professor of Finance at M.I.T.'s Alfred P. Sloan School of Management, who was my adviser in the preparation of this study from start to finish. I owe thanks to Miss Helen G. Grant, my secretary, for her tireless and dedicated efforts in preparing the several drafts of this book. Lastly, I am thankful to Norvin W. McCoy, Mobil's Manager of Banking Relations, who has been a most effective devil's advocate since CASH ALPHA was first conceived and, in so being, has been of enormous help in its development.

Robert F. Calman

New York
September, 1967

CONTENTS

1 INTRODUCTION

1.1. What Is CASH ALPHA?

CASH ALPHA is a linear program model for allocating levels of activity
within a company's banking system. Incorporated in the model are the details
of the company's agreements with its banks on (1) the price of specific services
performed by the banks and (2) the forms of compensation for those services.
Also incorporated in the model are company policies (or "over-all constraints")
with respect to individual banks (for example, average net collected balances
in Bank A should not be lower than $500 thousand) and with respect to all
of its banks, treated as a single banking *system*. Using a high-speed digital
computer, the CASH ALPHA model provides *best* solutions for firms with
banking systems of sufficient complexity such that optimal resource
allocation decisions (for instance, on which banks to disburse) for the
system as a whole are not obvious.

The key banking policy of many, if not a majority of business firms, will
deal with the company's banking system as a *source of credit* for both
presently identifiable and presently unidentifiable needs. In the example of
the hypothetical company ("Ancama Corporation") used in this book, key
company policy is to maintain the ability to borrow $50 million from its
banks on short notice (in addition to its established lines and outstanding
loans) to take advantage of unforseen investment opportunities or to
finance unanticipated major cash shortfalls. The reason that a firm uses

CASH ALPHA (the *objective function* of the CASH ALPHA linear program) is to minimize the cost to the company of its banking system, within policy constraints, while meeting the specific terms of each agreement with each of its banks.

A schematic diagram of the relationship of the objection function, over-all constraints, constraints existing at each bank in the system (such as the specific credit/charge arrangement between Ancama and each of the banks) and levels of activities is shown in Figure 1.1.

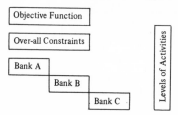

Figure 1.1. Schematic diagram of linear program relationships in CASH ALPHA.

1.2. Why CASH ALPHA?

CASH ALPHA is of value to a company with a banking system of sufficient complexity such that optimum resource allocation decisions for the system as a whole at any one time are not obvious. In Ancama Corporation, the hypothetical firm used as an example in this study, there are fifteen banks, each providing a different combination of services. The company receives monthly account-analysis statements from eight of the fifteen banks, and each of the eight differs in terms of the prices charged for services, on the service credit allowed on average demand deposit balances, and (in some cases) on tax payments made through the banks. Prior to adoption of CASH ALPHA, Ancama Corporation followed a policy of minimizing the cost of each banking relationship taken on its own terms – that is, of optimizing the *components* of the banking system. Variables open to Ancama each month (such as which banks should be used for disbursement and which banks should receive tax payments) were determined with the general objective of cost minimization. But little effort was directed toward optimizing the system as a whole, except in terms of providing what was felt to be an adequate call on credit.

The CASH ALPHA linear programming model, in contrast, treats all banks as components of a single system, subject to the actual terms of agreements between the firm and each of its banks. The power of this systems approach is demonstrated in Chapter 3, when CASH ALPHA is successfully used to reduce the cost of the system (as defined there) by over 30 per cent.

CASH ALPHA can be used by the company treasurer as a short-term planning mechanism. By feeding into the computer data on the levels of activities expected during a given month, the program (which integrates all the policy positions that the treasurer has made specific) furnishes an optimal solution for the allocation of activities. For example, it will show on which banks disbursements should be made, and in what quantities, and it will show where to target average balances for each bank, as reflected in the firm's own cash ledger, so that net collected balances at each bank will closely approximate a predetermined policy level.

But perhaps more important than its use as a short-term planning device in an ongoing system is CASH ALPHA's potential in the restructuring of a banking system. CASH ALPHA provides data for analysis by the treasurer in the form of marginal costs (or "shadow prices") of services provided by each of a firm's banks. (This is explained in some detail in Section 3.2 of Chapter 3). The treasurer can combine analysis of the CASH ALPHA output with his own knowledge of feasible changes to develop insights into the ways in which the structure of the system, or certain key policies, might be altered. With high-speed computing equipment, the treasurer can then test quickly and cheaply the economic consequences of alternate structures. Several structural changes are explored in Chapters 3 and 4, the most important of which are the two heuristic tests of lock-box bank[1] selection.

---

[1] A firm uses "lock-box banking" to lessen the time necessary to collect customer remittances. A firm, Company A, would establish a lock-box in a post office convenient to its bank, to which Company A's customers would be asked to direct their remittances. The bank would have access to the lock-box. It would empty the box several times a day, bringing the mail back to the bank for processing. At the bank, envelopes would be emptied, and checks separated from return cards and other matter. Unless a check failed to meet tests established by Company A, the bank would immediately put the check into the clearing process. Return slips or cards, any checks that failed to meet Company A's tests, and any correspondence sent in by Company A's customers would be forwarded each day to Company A by the bank. In some cases, the bank might partially process return cards (by sorting them into order) or it might make a magnetic tape of the day's processing (excluding irregular items) and forward the taped data by dataphone to the customer's computer center. A firm might establish lock-box arrangements with banks in several of its distribution areas. A firm benefits from using a lock-box arrangement through the acceleration of the collection of receivables (which results from the elimination of handling time by the company's accounting office from the work flow in the case of normal items) and it also benefits because a portion of the clerical work that would normally take place in its accounting office is being performed by the bank. Banks are normally compensated for lock-box services through the earnings implicit in deposit balances maintained with them by lock-box customers, or through cash fees, or through the earnings implicit in federal excise, withholding, or income taxes paid through them. In common banking usage, a "retail" lock-box is one in which the individual remittance handled has a value of $100 or less: a "wholesale" lock-box is one in which the individual remittance handled has a value of $1,000 or more — those between $100 and $1,000 may be classified as either "retail" or "wholesale," depending on the bank. In a "wholesale" lock-box arrangement, it is often common for a Xerox (or similar) copy of the remittance check to be made for the bank customer's records.

1.3. A Firm's Investment in Cash

The objective in the CASH ALPHA linear program reflects the different costs to the company of different forms of compensation it can use to pay its banks for services rendered. I differentiate among four classes of compensation: (1) average deposit balances created by a continuing cash level on a company's own cash ledger, (2) average deposit balances created by disbursing activity, a kind of "float," (3) cash fees, and (4) tax payments made through the banks. In the objective function, I assign a zero cost to the company of tax payments and balances created by disbursing, because these actions would have to be taken even if there were no costs associated with bank services. The cost of cash fees is obviously equal to the amount paid. I assign a cost of 20 per cent per year, before federal income taxes, to average company cash ledger balances. The 20 per cent figure is a pretax equivalent of the cost-of-capital for a firm that estimates its after-tax cost-of-capital at 10 per cent. The cost-of-capital concept is not absolutely vital for use of CASH ALPHA. A cost factor for average company cash ledger balances equivalent to current short-term money market rates — perhaps the most current rate for ninety-day Treasury bills or bank Certificates of Deposit — could be used as well as a cost-of-capital factor, from a *computational* standpoint. In testing the sensitivity of the value of cash in connection with the hypothetical company, I found that the shifts in banking activity that took place when moving down from a 20 per cent rate to a short-term portfolio security rates were quite small. The reason is that as long as money market rates are higher than the earnings credit allowed by the banks, there exists a powerful economic drive within CASH ALPHA to minimize investment in cash balances. Before proceeding into CASH ALPHA, I think there is value in taking a short detour and investigating the "cost" of investment in cash by a company.

1.4. A Digression on the Cost of Cash

Despite the popularity of cost-of-capital concepts among financial managers for use on a wide variety of investment decisions, the opportunity cost for cash balances is probably viewed more often by bankers (and company treasurers) as the current rate available on short-term money market investments. For example, Furniss and Nadler suggest that the steady rise in interest rates over the past ten years has been a major economic drive in the paring of bank balances by major corporations, which suggests that financial managers as a group assign an opportunity cost to cash equal to short-term money market obligations.[2] The slow growth of demand

[2] James P. Furniss and Paul S. Nadler, "Should Banks Reprice Corporate Services?" *Harvard Business Review* Vol. 44, No. 3 (May-June 1966), p. 99.

deposits in the banking system during the past several years in contrast with the growth of the total money supply, and in particular the growth of time deposits, seems ample evidence that such an economic drive has existed. But to accept such a cost concept is to deny the validity of an opportunity cost for the company as a whole. That such an over-all opportunity cost exists is evident from a study of many companies' investment program decisions.

Although a company may well have available to it significant unused credit capacity, it will reject investment proposals that fall below what it determines to be its cost-of-capital. The existence of significant unused credit capacity, particularly in an industry in which capital is felt to be the major constraint on increased earnings, should be viewed as a transient situation as a company evolves toward what it believes is an optimal capital structure. This evolution takes time. In the meantime, a firm may reject temporarily investment proposals that are expected to yield returns in excess of its cost-of-capital on a risk-weighted basis rather than add new debt — by expanding its financing, especially borrowings, at a rate that a number of its creditors might feel imprudent. Whenever capital is rationed, divestment decisions of whatever nature should, in my opinion, be considered as the source of capital that can be reinvested in the business at the company's cost-of-capital. On this basis, a reduction of cash would enable the company to expand its capital programs. It matters little that the cash passes through the short-term investment portfolio. This is a way station for *all* divestment funds, whether they emanate from a decrease in cash balances or from the sale of a surplus property.

An argument is sometimes made that a firm has a fixed minimum need for liquid funds, and thus within the cash/short-term investment pool the opportunity cost is simply the current short-term money market rate. Recent years have shown that many firms that had historically maintained short-term investment portfolios as their prime source of liquidity (and avoided short-term bank debt at the end of their fiscal years) have shifted to a position of using their short-term borrowing potential at their banks as their apparent prime source of liquidity. So the fixed-minimum-need argument seems to me to have limited validity.

Even if one adopts the fixed-minimum-need argument and assigns a money market opportunity cost for decisions relating to the composition of the sum of balances at a firm's major credit-granting banks and the funds invested in short-term portfolio securities, the cost-of-capital basis would still seem appropriate for many banking system decisions. For example, if a firm compensated a bank providing lock-box services exclusively with balances, then its investment in cash in that bank would tend to be frozen if lock-box activity remained constant, and would grow if lock-box activity increased. Even if such a bank charged less for the service rendered than the firm could obtain elsewhere, and even if the bank allowed an earnings credit on average balances that was fully equivalent to short-term money market rates, the decision to utilize such a lock-box might be nonoptimal for the firm if the firm is engaged in capital rationing. To use such a bank involves an *investment* decision, in terms of cash balances, as well as an operating decision. I do not argue that the choice of such a lock-box is *necessarily* nonoptimal for a firm in capital rationing. The key, I believe, is the firm's potential use of the bank as a source of credit. If for some reason the bank is not competent or interested in credits in the firm's industry, or the firm simply does not look to that bank for credit, then the rules I have adopted for CASH ALPHA would show the relationship to be nonoptimal. But if the bank is a potential and interested lender in support of the firm's activities, the firm's needs for credit potential may make the relationship attractive.

CASH ALPHA, as used in the example later in this study, implicitly states that a firm will want a liquidity reserve in the form of borrowing potential with its banks. Because of this need for a reserve, the firm will maintain balances with its banks that give it an effective call on borrowings. Beyond the point of maintaining this liquidity reserve, there is little value to a firm in carrying added balances with its banks, except when a required service — tangible or intangible — can be acquired from the banks only through balances or through a combination of balances and other forms of compensation. The short-term investment portfolio, in my opinion, serves as a *decoupling mechanism* between a firm's investment in cash and its investment in other assets. It is *not* primarily a liquidity base, although, obviously, when a short-term portfolio exists it also serves in that function.

1.5. The Price of Bank Services

The price charged for tangible services by a bank may or may not affect the cost of that relationship to the firm. If the firm maintains large balances with a bank with the essential purpose of having a call on credit, but does not require much in the way of tangible services from the bank, then the schedule of service charges is a matter of little concern to the company. The relationship of the mythical Ancama Corporation, with the equally mythical Second National Bank of New York is a good illustration of this. As a matter of policy, Ancama keeps net collected balances with this bank equal to (1) 15 per cent of average loans outstanding, plus (2) 10 per cent of average unused lines (both on a six-month moving average basis), plus (3) $1 million. The last $1 million serves, Ancama feels, as a call on credit for unforeseen cash needs. One result of this policy is that, because of loans and its credit line, Ancama carries net collected balances with the Second National in excess of $3 million. Ancama pays dividends on this bank, and also draws some of its normal monthly headquarters payment checks on it. But total tangible activity amounts to only about five thousand checks paid per month. Ancama does not request a monthly statement analysis from the bank. If it did, and if the bank allowed 5 per cent on "available for investment" balances[3] and charged 5¢ per check, as does the National Bank of Chicago, Ancama's "bench-mark" bank, then the service-charge credit would be about $11,000, but the price of tangible services would total only about $250, for an "excess profit" from balances alone of $10,750. If the bank increased its normal schedule of prices for services performed, Ancama would not increase its balances.

Consider another example: the bank that is performing essentially a collection and data-processing service for the company. Ancama has a relationship with the U.S. National Bank of California, a bank that has not participated in any loans to the company. Its essential function to Ancama is to process retail lock-box items — about 55,100 per month. The bank's price for this activity is 3.4¢ per item. It allows a service-charge credit of 3.875 per cent on available-for-investment balances, or about 3.25 per cent on net collected balances. At one time Ancama maintained sufficient net collected balances with this bank to offset the price of tangible services rendered with service-charge credit on balances. Growing balances with this bank, due solely to increased lock-box activity, led Ancama to the use of tax payments as a method of compensating the bank in part for its services. (See Appendix B.16 for the details of Ancama's agreement with this bank.)

A word should be said about the price and service-charge credit schedules I have used in the Ancama Corporation example. They are not "real" in the sense that any one of them reflects the actual slate of charges in effect at any one bank that I know of. Probably both the service-charge level and the price level are higher than normal, but the *combination* of service charge level and price is not radically out of line with the practice of many banks. That is, the bank that allows a 2.5 per cent earnings allowance on net collected balances and charges 3¢ per retail lock-box item is on the same economic level as the bank that allows 5 per cent earnings on net collected balances and charges 6¢ per retail lock-box item. In any case, my purpose here is *not* to make an argument for any particular level of service-charge credits or prices. Rather, it is to demonstrate the versatility of CASH ALPHA in handling a variety of combinations of compensation and charges so as to meet the conditions of each company/bank agreement while also meeting

[3] I use the expression "available for investment" balances in this paper to mean net collected balances less reserve requirements on those balances.

the goal of minimizing cost to the company within the policy constraints that are in effect at the time the program is run.

A word should also be said perhaps about "prices." Many banks refer to their per-item charges as "costs" rather than prices. When this is done, an argument is often made that the bank should earn a profit beyond its stated "costs." This leaves up to the customer the question as to what *level* of profit the bank should earn. In many cases this is no problem. For example, Ancama is not concerned with the analysis statement profitability of its relationship with the Second National Bank of New York — it does not even ask for an analysis statement. Its interest is in maintaining a call on credit with this bank, and so it maintains large balances, which may be misinterpreted by some as overgenerous compensation for intangible services performed.

But how about the banks that do not enjoy these seemingly excess balances? Should the financial management of a company calculate what it feels to be the proper level of "profit" for its banks? If so, a major practical problem for company financial management is the degree of comparability of "costs" among banks. While it is obvious that costs must be higher in some banks than in others, the range of data that is said to reflect costs, in the form of bank analysis statements, is so broad that there is room for healthy skepticism on the part of company financial management as to the validity of any "cost" data furnished to it. In some cases it appears that these data may be little more than marginal cost figures. In others, the "costs" seem to be loaded with every imaginable overhead item in the bank, plus an implicit profit factor. The company financial officer who sees several of these every month cannot help but be suspect of "costs" as a figure to which he should arbitrarily add a "profit" element. It seems to me that company financial management must consider analysis statement data essentially as a slate of *prices* (some banks do), and the company must meet this slate of prices if it is to do business with that bank. This is not to say that the company should neglect the intangible services provided by the bank. The level of balances maintained at a major credit-supplying bank (such as the Second National of New York in Ancama's case) may suffice to compensate the bank for intangible services. Also, the level of prices charged for tangibles by a bank may be so loaded with implicit profit that the bank is willing to provide intangible services even on an analysis statement break-even basis. However, in many cases it should be proper for company financial management to add a factor to the compensation level agreed upon for tangibles so as to provide for intangibles.

The best bank-customer relationship, in my opinion, is one in which a bank provides services for its customer that it can provide better or cheaper than the customer can provide for itself, and in which the customer compensates the bank equitably for the services performed. A banking relationship need

not be cut to the bone to be cost effective. But the reverse is also true: one
need not abandon cost effectiveness to have good banking relations. Few
bankers would argue that their major corporate customers should be less
sophisticated in cash management than the banks themselves are. Most
would, I believe, join with Charles A. Agemian, Executive Vice President
of The Chase Manhattan Bank, N.A., in recognizing the corporate financial
manager's responsibility to manage his company's investment in cash.
Agemian wrote: "Please do not think that I am critical of the corporate
treasurer's cash management program. So long as the bank is being
compensated for services rendered, so long as the company maintains
adequate supporting balances for lines of credit, and so long as it recognizes
the hundreds of services available for its benefit and compensates the bank
for this use, no banker can complain."[4] Agemian goes on to say that the
banker can present a convincing case for keeping excess capital in the form
of bank balances, and maintains that the better planned financial decisions
are made when a bank loan rather than a short-term investment portfolio
is the financing mechanism for providing needed funds. While I believe
the opportunity cost of bank balances is *not* the short-term portfolio
investment rate, as Agemian implies, I agree with him on the value of
the banks as the important source of financial flexibility for the company,
and I would perhaps go beyond this to say that in most cases this is the
key factor for a mutually attractive relationship.

1.6. Dual Use of Average Balances

In using CASH ALPHA, I assume that a dollar of net collected balances
can serve a dual purpose: first, to serve as "compensating" balances for
negotiated credit arrangements and as a call on additional credit, and
second, to pay for tangible or intangible services. Returning to the
example of Ancama Corporation and the Second National Bank of
New York, there appeared to be about $10,750 of "excess profits"
per month based on tangible services and the value of net collected
balances. But Ancama also received valuable intangible services from the
Second National. It calculated that these services had a value to it of
$78,000 per year, or $6,500 per month. Thus there were still "excess
profits" to the bank occasioned by Ancama's desire to maintain a major
call on credit with this bank.

One might argue that a dollar of deposits *should not* serve as both a
call on credit and as compensation for services. In some cases, banks are
probably able to separate the two. Some large users of bank credit, such

---

[4]Charles A. Agemian, "Maintaining an Effective Bank Relationship," *Financial Executive* (January 1964) p. 24.

as sales finance and small loan companies, maintain some banking relationships that call for little or no check processing, or similar tangible services, and essentially no intangible services. The *entire* relationship in such cases revolves around the availability of credit. And yet these relationships are, I believe, the exception to the rule. Agemian describes what is probably the more typical case: "This brings us to the rather complex problem of 'compensating balances' or 'supporting balances' as I prefer to call them. These balances are not a clear addition to the cost of credit, and the examples used exaggerate the effect in the vast majority of cases. First of all, a borrower is almost always a depositor, and as such is required by his own operating, liquidity, or reserve needs to maintain a cash balance at some bank. And, generally speaking, the level of these balances is enough to constitute supporting balances!"[5]

Whether balances can serve a dual purpose or not is a matter for bank-customer negotiation. In either case, CASH ALPHA can be used by the company in determining optimal allocation of variables within the system. In the Ancama example I have provided for dual use of balances, which seems to me to be almost universally the rule today. One implication of dual use is that, all other things being equal, it pays a company to concentrate tangible activity (and intangibles as well) at those banks where the company expects to borrow, and thus make maximum use of its balances at such banks. As a corollary, a company would tend to make every effort to develop an understanding of potential credit needs with well-sited regional collection banks, so that it could gain the value of quicker collection of receivables, without increasing its investment in cash, by making use of the regional banks for lock-box activity and as important elements in the firm's reservoir of potential credit.

1.7. The Price of Intangible Services

Implicit in every balance level decision made by a major firm is a price for intangible services rendered. It may or may not be the result of a deliberate attempt to add up the value of all the intangible services provided by the banks. But whether deliberate or not, an allowance — perhaps an allowance of zero — is in fact made when a company determines a balance level at a bank.

I think that a company *should* make an effort to add up the value of the intangibles it seeks and receives from its banks. Some are relatively easy to calculate. A bank may take on a research job similar to what might be done by an independent consultant (for example, a major international bank might undertake a survey of potential licensees for

[5]*Ibid.*, p. 25.

a product in a foreign country), and, based on the quality of the job and a knowledge of consultants' fees, an approximation can be made of the value of the bank's service. A bank may make a special effort to acquaint new employees transferred to a company facility in the bank's town with many aspects of community life there. While far from precise, a per capita value of such a service can be assigned. A bank might have a regional new-business scouting service that funnels news and rumors about local business developments to its customers. One speciality that virtually every bank has for "sale," and which is difficult to duplicate, is its intimate knowledge of business conditions in its own local area.

Some intangibles are very difficult to price. Examples are the value of an idea furnished by an imaginative banker who has followed a company's fortunes closely for many years and developed valuable insights in the company's business, or an acquisition proposal, or aid in locating executive talent. But the difficulty of the pricing job does not eliminate the need to do it. As unsatisfactory as the estimates may seem to be, there is value in the exercise, I believe, if only to identify which banks are consistently providing such services. There is probably equal value to a bank in adding up the intangible services it provides to its important customers and in seeing how the totals compare with the compensation it is getting from those customers!

I think there is as great a danger in banking as in industry that talent will be diverted to unrewarding tasks. Thus a bank may invest the time of its people in providing intangibles that the customer — particularly the major company customer — simply cannot use. Drucker describes the following example of a technical service group, which might well fit the national accounts division of a major bank:

A large engineering company prided itself on the high quality and reputation of its technical service group, which contained several hundred expensive men. The men were indeed first-rate. But analysis of their allocation showed clearly that they, while working hard, contributed little. Most of them worked on the "interesting" problems — especially those of the very small customers — problems which, even if solved produced little, if any, business. The automobile industry is the company's major customer and accounts for almost one-third of all purchases. But few technical service people, within anyone's memory had even set foot in the engineering department or the plant of an automobile company. "General Motors and Ford don't need us; they have their own people," was their reaction.[6]

In the Ancama example I have included a section on intangible values in the descriptive material on each bank (Appendixes B.1 through B.19) but

[6]Peter F. Drucker, "Managing for Business Effectiveness," *Harvard Business Review* Vol. 41, No. 3 (May-June 1963), p. 55.

I have excluded explicit values in the CASH ALPHA model. In the model, intangibles are supported by balances that have a primary function as a call on credit in some cases, and intangibles form the basis for minimum balance constraints in others. For example, in the latter category are three factory-town banks that provide little in the way of tangible services to Ancama. When Ancama centralized much of its banking activity in the recent (mythical) past, it was felt necessary to maintain a "good" relationship with banks in these towns for the many kinds of support given to local management. It was decided rather arbitrarily to maintain a $250 thousand balance at one of these banks. Although the company would have had trouble explaining the economic justification for such a decision, this balance level just seemed right to those concerned, although no one was willing to say that the relationship was necessarily *worth* $50 thousand per year — the balance level times the company's opportunity cost of 20 per cent.

CASH ALPHA handles this simply by constraining net collected balances at this bank at or above the $250 thousand level. Thus a computerized planning system such as CASH ALPHA can integrate, with no particular problem, those subjective decision situations that every firm probably faces with one or many of its banks.

1.8.   Operations Research and Its Use in Cash Administration

Over the past twenty years the use by business of various new quantitative methods of analysis has grown, particularly in the management of manufacturing operations and distribution systems. Linear and dynamic programming, multiple regression analysis and multiple correlation analysis, PERT and CPM, exponentially—weighted smoothed forecasts. Bayesian statistical decision making — all are tools that are being used increasingly to solve management problems. Perhaps somewhat inaccurately, all of these methods are often lumped together under the heading "operations research" or "management science," described by Simon as

> . . . a movement that, emerging out of the military needs of World War II, has brought the decision-making problems of management within the range of interests of large numbers of natural scientists and, particularly, of mathematicians and statisticians. The operations researchers soon joined forces with mathematical economists who had come into the same area — to the mutual benefit of both groups. And by now there has been widespread fraternization between these exponents of the "new" scientific management and men trained in the earlier traditions of scientific management and industrial engineering. No meaningful line can be drawn any more to demarcate operations research from

scientific management or scientific management from management science.[7]

A key concept in understanding operations research is the "systems approach" point of view. Simon describes it as follows: "At its vaguest, it means looking at the whole problem — again, hardly a novel idea, and not always a very helpful one. Somewhat more concretely, it means designing the components of a system and making individual decisions within it in the light of the implication of these decisions for the system as a whole."[8]

The growth of operations research has followed the growth of computer usage in data-processing applications. Increased electronic data processing (EDP) applications have lowered the cost of computer time, which has in turn increased the practicality of using the computer for operations research activities.

What now appears to be revolutionary is the growing use of the new analytical methods and the computer by *managers* familiar with these techniques in decision making. A growing body of managers not only knows these new tools but can recognize that these tools may be profitably employed in solving the problems of the various business specialties. This in no way lessens the value of the professional operations researcher. A powerful management combination is provided by a manager with training in these techniques working closely with a staff specialist who is a professional operations researcher.

Many of the problems now being worked on are so complex that a direct solution is impossible. In such cases, simulation techniques are useful. A mathematical model is built of a system, and a manager can test possible alternatives on the model, much as an aeronautical engineer can test different wing shapes in a wind tunnel. The selection of *which* alternatives to test in these complex problems that are not capable of direct solution remains a matter of managerial "mystique." The process of picking out possible ways of improving a system and then testing them by simulation is called "heuristic testing."

CASH ALPHA is a relatively simple use of one such quantitative technique — linear programming — both for a problem-solving application and for heuristic testing. In its first role, CASH ALPHA enables the financial manager to make optimal decisions on the allocation of variables (where to disburse, where to make tax payments, where to pay fees) in the short run. In its second role, CASH ALPHA is of value

[7]Herbert A. Simon, *The Shape of Automation for Men and Management* (New York: Harper & Row, Publishers, 1965), p. 69.

[8]*Ibid.*, pp. 69-70.

in showing the financial manager where his marginal costs are particularly high, so he can direct renegotiation effort there, and where his marginal costs are low, so he can direct additional business there. But perhaps more important to the firm, CASH ALPHA can be used as a model to test the effect of changes in a firm's system of lock-box banks.

There is a difference between CASH ALPHA and the normal simulation model. "Simulation" normally denotes the handling of a problem that is sufficiently complex so that direct solution is impossible. Rather than "solve" a problem, we construct a mathematical model of a situation, feed it simulated or historical data, and then test alternate components of the model to see which components work better than others. "Heuristics" is the term employed to describe the process by which the problem solver utilizes his knowledge of the situation, his experience, and rules of thumb that have proved successful in the past to determine *which* components to vary. The end result of a simulation problem is a series of case studies, each of which provides answers to what might logically have happened in the real-world system described by the model.

CASH ALPHA, a linear programming model, represents a large number of alternative components simultaneously. The solution is a *non*heuristic determination of the best of these alternative components. But heuristics come in when the financial manager selects the particular *set* of alternative components to be defined by the model. The set he selects is only one subset of the universe of all possible subsets of alternatives. Thus, in its "simulation" role, CASH ALPHA renders precise solutions to different sets of alternative components, sets which are heuristically determined by the financial manager.

Some work has been done in applying operations research techniques to finance, although the field seems to be in its infancy. Some of the most interesting work has been done in security portfolio selection by institutional trustees and in the setting of competitive bidding strategies by security underwriters. The banks themselves, which have been leading users of computers for EDP applications, increasingly are hiring operations researchers and using these techniques themselves, and in some cases are offering such services to their customers. Thus there should be little surprise on the part of bankers in developments such as CASH ALPHA.

2 THE ANCAMA CORPORATION CASE STUDY

2.1. Ancama Corporation

Ancama Corporation is a mythical manufacturer of a product that is sold nationally to wholesale and retail users. Annual sales are about $420 million. Ancama has a subsidiary that manages Ancama's investment in foreign subsidiaries, affiliates, and licensees. Its international banking relations, however, are not included in this example, except for the intangible service value that Ancama receives in support of its international operations from one bank and except for the balances that the subsidiary carries with this bank. CASH ALPHA could be expanded for global operations, but for simplicity's sake I have kept the Ancama example essentially a domestic operation. Ancama banks with fifteen mythical banks.

Ancama has its headquarters in New York City. It has three regional accounting centers — in Boston, Chicago, and San Francisco — that provide accounting and other services for Ancama's manufacturing and sales operations. The accounting centers administer relations with the banks in their regions in accordance with policy guidelines established by Ancama's financial management in New York. Appendix A summarizes Ancama's average balances, average monthly tax payments, and the value of services performed for Ancama by the banks. In addition, summaries of Ancama's dealings with each of these banks, and the policy guidelines set for each, are included in Appendixes B.1 through B.19. Also, a schematic diagram of Ancama's banking relations, with mnemonics used later in this study, is contained in Appendix C.

Ancama uses its short-term investment portfolio, and to a lesser extent its lines of credit with the New York banks, as a "buffer" for day-to-day changes in cash. Funds are normally not accumulated in any regional bank. Rather, each day the accounting center cash manager trims those accounts that are used to collect receivables by wiring excess funds to other banks on which disbursements are made and by wiring any excess over that amount to one of the New York banks. Should the day's disbursement needs require cash from headquarters to supplement regional collections, the accounting center cash manager would request a wire transfer, or transfers, from the New York head-quarters as needed. Accumulation of funds in a bank administered by the accounting center normally takes place only when average net collected balances are running below the level required by policy or by agreement between Ancama and the bank.

A monthly cash forecast is made by each accounting center cash manager. It is used by Ancama's financial staff in New York to set short-term invest-ment and borrowing strategy. In addition, the accounting center cash manager normally advises Ancama's New York financial staff of significant shifts from forecast when such shifts become evident.

As the individual summaries on each bank show (Appendixes B.1 through B.19), a wide variety of service-charge/credit formulas exists among Ancama's banks. The National Bank of Chicago is a "bench-mark" bank for Ancama, because its schedule of earnings credit and charges is cheaper (for Ancama) than most, and because Ancama uses it both as a major provider of tangible services and as an important source of credit. There are banks that do not prepare monthly analysis statements for Ancama, because the company has not requested them. Thus, in such cases there are no meaningful formulas for tangibles. These banks – the major New York City banks and the three main plant-town banks – are thought to provide significant intangible services and, in the case of the New York banks, a critically important "call" on credit. The analysis earnings provided by average net collected balances with these banks far outweigh the price of tangible services performed. For example, earnings on deposit at the Second National Bank of New York far exceed the price of tangible services, as was demonstrated in Section 1.5. At the other extreme, is the Philadelphia Trust Company, which does an efficient, low-cost job of collect-ing retail lock-box items in the Middle Atlantic area, but is used for almost no other purpose by Ancama. In the case of this bank, changes in charges are of great importance, as they would change the level of balances required by the bank.

The "cost" of the banking system that Ancama maintains may be looked at from at least two perspectives. On the simpler level, it is the sum of the charges levied by the banks for tangible services, as shown in columns 7 and 8 of Appendix A. Certainly a company is obligated to compensate the banks for services rendered. One could add the value of intangible services, as shown in column 9, to the sum of tangibles.

But, more generally, the "cost" of the system is the opportunity cost of the cash that Ancama has more of less permanently invested in its banking system. The cash in the system does not provide liquidity *directly*. It does so only indirectly in its support of lines of credit and its support of a "call" on credit. Day-to-day needs are met chiefly through liquidation of securities in the firm's short-term investment portfolio, or by loans from line banks, *not* by drawing down significantly on the balances maintained with banks throughout the system. So in a very real sense the company's investment in cash is a fixed asset that is "current" by accounting definition only. What quantities does Ancama have invested in cash? Appendix A shows three figures, all of which are "cash balances" — company ledger balances, gross bank ledger balances, and net collected balances. The important one from the company's standpoint is the first one, company ledger balances, because a reduction in the required amount of this asset category allows investment in other assets. This is not to say that the company is not interested in net collected balances, the item of greatest interest to the banks. The net collected balance figure is the key one in determining the earnings credit used to pay for tangible services and in determining the company's call on credit. There is no economic difference to a bank in having a $1 million net collected balance that is the result of a dormant $1 million on its customer's cash ledger, and a $1 million balance that is entirely the result of float[1] created by the payment of checks on the bank. In either case it has $1 million, less reserve requirements, available for investment. In terms of the services it requires from two banks, each enjoying $1 million of net collected balances — but arising from the two sources noted — there is no need for the company to make any distinctions because of the *source* of the net collected balances. It is only in a consideration of the total system that company cash ledger balances, as a total for the entire system, become significant. There is, I think, danger of misinterpretation of the value of a company's relationship with its banks if it focuses attention on company ledger balances at any individual bank or banks. Let us consider a simple example. If a company's banking system consisted of only two banks — Bank A and Bank B — and the company's policy is to maintain $1 million in net collected balances with each bank, then it might maintain a dormant $1 million with Bank A, and a zero ledger balance with Bank B, but disburse $5 million per month on this latter bank, which disbursements (let us assume) would create $1 million of float. In this simple example, let us also assume no in-transit on deposits

---

[1]I am using "float" to define the difference between gross bank ledger balances and company ledger balances, and "checks-in-transit" or simply "in-transit" to define the difference between gross bank ledger balances and net collected balances. The latter is often referred to by bankers as "float," but I shall use the term "in-transit" throughout this study.

made in either bank. We now have a $1 million total on our company cash ledger, and $2 million in terms of average net collected balances on the banks' books. Let us change our policy: we want to reduce our investment in cash by $500 thousand. We could reduce our disbursements on Bank B from $5 million to $3.75 million, which would create only $750 thousand of float at that bank. The $1.25 million of disbursements diverted from Bank B could be disbursed on Bank A, creating float there of $250 thousand. We could then reduce our ledger balance at Bank A by $500 thousand, and average net collected balance at Bank A would be the sum of the $500 thousand remaining on our cash ledger plus the $250 thousand generated by float, for a total of $750 thousand. Each bank saw its net collected balances go down by $250 thousand even though the entire decrease in terms of company cash ledger balances came from Bank A. The $250 thousand per bank reduction in earning assets reflects the economic reality of the situation. To say that the savings in cash are attributable simply to the reduction of cash at Bank A would ignore this reality.

Appendix A shows two figures for the monthly cost of maintaining Ancama's banking system, one based on a 10 per cent after-tax cost-of-capital factor, and the other based on a 6 per cent pretax cost-of-money factor. In the cost-of-capital case, I have "grossed up" the 10 per cent rate to a pretax rate of 20 per cent per year, or 1.6667 per cent per month. The *system* thus costs Ancama, before income taxes, $168,070.03 per month on a cost-of-capital basis, or $50,420.00 per month on a 6 per cent cost-of-money basis. As we shall see, CASH ALPHA can help reduce this significantly. Although I have a strong preference for the cost-of-capital approach, CASH ALPHA does not require its users to be ardent advocates of cost-of-capital concepts. For some concerns – insurance companies, perhaps – opportunity cost would be a money market rate of one kind or another. My own feeling is that a systems approach to banking, such as CASH ALPHA, produces its best results when the cost-of-capital approach is used to determine *structure* but a cost-of-money factor is used to determine month-to-month actions pending structural change.

2.2. Analysis of Ancama's Banking Structure

Ancama's management was not satisfied with the return it was earning on its investment in cash. Based on the Appendix A figures, it looked as though Ancama was getting about $15 thousand worth of tangible value and another $19 thousand worth of intangible value every month from its banking system (excluding the value of the call on credit). When this amount was related to the $10.1 million of cash that Ancama had, on average, on its books, it came to only about 3.4 per cent per year *before* taxes. Even if the intangible services furnished by the banks (excluding for the time being the value of its call on additional credit) were worth twice what the company estimated, the return would amount to only about 5.3 per cent before taxes.

Not only was the company's investment in cash earnings a low return, it was also growing to provide earnings credit sufficient to offset the large service charges at Ancama's five retail lock-box banks (in Boston, Philadelphia, Chicago, Dallas, and Los Angeles), which were handling more items each year.

Ancama did not need a $10 million investment in company cash ledger balances merely to process checks. This vital function could be performed quite adequately with a much smaller investment in cash. The intangible services afforded by the banks were appreciated, but with the exception of the major plant-town banks, it was difficult to rationalize a permanent investment in cash to pay for the advice it was getting. But the key factor, Ancama reasoned, was the potential need that it might have for credit. At the time of the analysis of its banking structure – early 1967 – Ancama had lines of credit totaling $25 million with the three New York banks. In addition, $5.95 million was owing to the three New York and two Chicago banks on a ten-year term loan made to Ancama International, Inc., a wholly owned subsidiary, and $700 thousand owing to one of the New York banks on another term loan made to Ancama Ajax, Inc., another wholly owned subsidiary.

Beyond its lines, which Ancama regularly used during the year, and the term loans, Ancama's management saw value in having an effective "call" on borrowed money. It felt that the maximum financing need that the company could reasonably predict was $50 million, about the largest acquisition that Ancama would attempt on a cash purchase basis. If it wanted to acquire a larger concern, management felt, it would probably do so through an exchange of shares, or through the issuance of some form of securities in a part-cash, part-securities transaction. A requirement of $50 million would probably not be all financed by banks. It seemed far more likely that about half of such an amount would be financed by institutional investors. Thus the most reasonable "maximum" need that management could predict $25 million from the banks. And to have a call on this amount, Ancama felt, it would need to keep $2.5 million with key banks in its system beyond the balances needed to support outstanding term loans and lines. Ancama recognized the problems inherent in such a broad projection, and also saw the possibility that temporary money market conditions might make it unattractive to seek institutional credit at some future date. Thus, exhibiting a penchant for safety factors, Ancama decided that it should target its call from the banks at $50 million, which would require, it felt, balances of $5 million over and above support for present lines and loans.

Ancama drew up a list to show where it wanted the $50 million of borrowing reserve to be. This is given in Table 2.1.

Table 2.1. Ancama's Borrowing Reserve

Bank	Potential Reserve (in millions of dollars)
Second National Bank, New York	$10.0
Wall Street Trust Company, New York	10.0
Merchants National Bank, New York	5.0
National Bank of Chicago	5.0
Third National Bank of Boston	5.0
U.S. National Bank of California	5.0
La Salle Street Trust Company	2.5
Union Trust Company, Los Angeles	2.0
Second National Bank, Dallas	2.0
Other banks	3.5
Total	$50.0

Management realized that by maintaining balances at the key New York banks at a level close to their historical levels — which the company also decided it would do — its borrowing potential would *exceed* the $50 million target. Thus, no one was concerned about the rather vague $3.5 million "other banks" category.

This borrowing reserve figure was *the key decision* in Ancama's banking structure analysis. From this basic, and somewhat subjective, decision flowed a whole series of decisions involving all aspects of Ancama's banking structure.

2.3. Collection Systems

Ancama used five banks to collect retail lock-box items. The five, their monthly volumes, the per-item analysis charge used by each, and a "fee-equivalent" per-item charge, are shown in Table 2.2. The "fee-equivalent" charge is based on an earnings credit roughly equivalent to short-term money market rates, and it is intended to represent that per-item charge at which each bank should be willing to accept fees in lieu of balances. In this example Ancama used the current ninety-day major bank Certificate of Deposit (C.D.) rate of 5 1/8 per cent. It is necessary to use something like a fee-equivalent in *comparing* banks because of the lack of uniformity among bank service-charge/credit formulas.

Table 2.2.   Ancama's Retail Lock-Box Bank Costs

Bank	Items Per Month	Per-Item Analysis Charge (in cents)	"Fee-equivalent" Analysis Charge* (in cents)
National Bank of Chicago	73,000	3.75	3.61
Third National Bank of Boston	33,600	3.0	6.03
Philadelphia Trust Company	23,800	3.5	4.02
Second National Bank of Dallas	42,500	4.5	6.02
U.S. National Bank of California	55,100	3.4	4.23
Total	228,000		

*Computed as follows:

$$\text{Per-item analysis charge} \times \frac{(\text{current 90-day C.D. rate}) \ (1 - \text{reserve requirement for time deposits})}{\text{bank analysis allowance on funds "available for investment"}}$$

For the Second National Bank of Dallas, the "fee-equivalent" analysis charge would be

$$4.5¢ \times \frac{(0.05125) \ (1 - 0.06)}{0.036} = 4.5¢ \times \frac{(0.05125) \ (0.94)}{0.036} = 4.5¢ \times \frac{(0.048175)}{0.036} =$$

$$4.5¢ \times 1.33819 = 6.02¢$$

Ancama's financial management recognized that bank costs could vary from city to city, but it did not feel that the spread on a fee-equivalent basis from 3.61¢ to 6.03¢ per item — the latter being about 67 per cent more expensive than the former — was justified. Nevertheless, the company had not, prior to this study, made a major effort to reduce the costs at the higher-priced banks.[2]

Ancama maintained five wholesale lock-boxes. Monthly volumes, per-item analysis charges, and fee-equivalent per-item charges, are shown in Table 2.3.

Table 2.3.   Ancama's Wholesale Lock-Box Bank Costs

Bank	Items per Month	Per-Item Analysis Charge (in cents)	"Fee-equivalent" Analysis Charge* (in cents)
National Bank of Chicago	5,100	6.5	6.27
La Salle Street Trust Company	7,900	5.0	9.63
Williams Trust Company	4,420	6.8	8.74
U.S. National Bank of California	3,060	6.2	7.71
Union Trust Company	4,870	6.5	9.63
Total	25,350		

[2] A "fee-equivalent" could also be based on tax payments, or on the particular combination of balances and tax payments that a bank is agreeable to, and not simply on balances, as I have used here.

Each accounting center normally received some checks in the mail each day that should have been mailed to the lock-box banks. These items, and other accounting center receipts, were deposited over the counter each day in a local bank, normally the major Ancama bank in that city. The cashier at headquarters made similar deposits in one of the New York banks each day.

2.4. Disbursements

In each accounting center there are three kinds of disbursing accounts: regular, payroll, and emergency. There is one payroll account bank for each accounting center. General disbursements can be made on all banks within the center's region, but normally are not made on the plant-town banks. For example, Chicago normally disburses on three banks, the National Bank of Chicago, the La Salle Street Trust Company, and the Second National Bank of Dallas. Emergency accounts are maintained at banks in Ancama's three plant towns for use by plant managers in case of unforeseen needs.

Ancama's New York banks are all used for general disbursements by headquarters. In addition, dividends are paid on the Second National Bank of New York, and the headquarters payroll account and the Ancama International, Inc., accounts are maintained at Wall Street Trust Company.

Disbursement decisions are made so as to compensate banks for tangible services performed in accordance with individual agreements between Ancama and the banks, or so as to maintain balances at predetermined policy levels.

2.5. Tax Payments

Federal excise, withholding, and income tax payments may be made directly to banks designated for that purpose by the U.S. Treasury Department in lieu of making such payments to the Treasury. A bank credits such payments to a "Treasury Tax and Loan Account" on its books. These payments are of great value to the banks, because the Treasury does not call on the full amount of the payments immediately; rather, a delayed call on these funds is made during the days following any particular tax payment date. The net result is that a bank may often receive fifteen to twenty days' (or more) use of these funds. The banks do not pay interest to the government on these funds, but they do maintain against them, as against any demand deposits, the normal reserve requirement on deposits with the Federal Reserve Banks.

The method of payment of taxes is discretionary as far as the taxpayer is concerned — he may pay excise taxes to Bank A or Bank B or directly to the Treasury — with no difference in tax cost. Because of the Treasury's practice of calling funds on a delayed basis, the banks compete aggressively for this business, some offering service-charge credit for tax payments made through them.

In Ancama's case, tax payments amounted to about $4 million per month. Ancama normally paid $625,000 per month of this to the U.S. National Bank of California, which allowed an earnings credit of $781.25 per month on this sum, equivalent to 3 per cent per annum on the $625,000 for fifteen days.[3] The balance of its tax payments Ancama had normally paid through the three New York banks for intangible services performed. However, the analysis made in connection with the CASH ALPHA study indicated that these tax payments were providing what appeared to be excessive compensation for New York banks, so Ancama's financial management determined to see whether these tax payments could be put to use to pay for tangible services, such as defrayment of the cost of maintaining lock-boxes.

2.6. Cash Fees

Prior to the CASH ALPHA study, Ancama did not pay cash fees to its banks for commercial banking services, although it had done so for many years in connection with transfer agency and registrarship charges, as well as with fees in connection with the bank-trusteed Ancama Pension Plan.

In the round of discussions with its banks in early 1967, Ancama sought quotes on the cash-fee basis on which some of the banks would provide services, and the banks that were asked to quote cash fees did so. Ancama was motivated to seek cash-fee quotes because of the high cost-of-capital it assigned to bank balances, particularly in those banks where Ancama did not seek a call on future borrowings. For example, although the Philadelphia Trust Company's retail lock-box charge was attractively priced, it was no particular bargain if Ancama could pay for that service only by "investing" in demand-deposit balances with this bank, while at the same time it was rationing capital and rejecting what appeared to be attractive investment opportunities. In this case the funds at Philadelphia Trust provided neither liquidity nor a wanted call on credit. They were simply a fixed investment in cash at a money-market yield.

2.7. The January 1967 Round of Negotiations

In January 1967, Ancama's treasurer held extensive discussions with most of Ancama's banks on the subject of service charges and the acceptability of tax payments and cash fees in lieu of demand balances. The results are shown in the individual bank summaries in Appendixes B.1 through B.19. The discussions focused on flexibility in the methods for compensating each bank each month.

[3] Or approximately 3.59 per cent on the average available for investment balances created by the $625,000 tax payment.

2.8. Writing CASH ALPHA Equations

At the conclusion of the January round of discussions, it was clear that there was no intuitively obvious best way to allocate variables in a typical month so as to minimize the cost of the banking system, consistent with maintenance of the $50 million borrowing reserve. Nor was it obvious how changes in monthly levels of variables might affect optimality. "Variables" in this case mean the allocation of disbursements, the allocation of tax payments, and the use of cash fees. Accordingly, it was decided to make a mathematical model of Ancama's banking system and utilize linear programming to determine the optimum allocation of variables. What linear programming does is to solve simultaneously several equations with several unknowns. This would be a tedious and time-consuming exercise were it not for high-speed electronic computers. Prior to the development of such computers, financial managers would have been limited by practicality to making an *estimate* of what was optimal. But with linear programming, the calculation of optimality is fast and simple; it is also cheap considering the savings achieved through the ability to calculate optimality.

To understand CASH ALPHA, it will be useful to review the *objective function* of the model and to analyze in some depth the equations used to define Ancama's relationship with one of its major-service banks.

2.9. CASH ALPHA's Objective Function

The objective function of any linear program model is that function of the independent variables whose maximum or minimum is sought in an optimization problem. In the case of CASH ALPHA, it is the single best combination of the division of disbursements, payment of taxes, and payment of cash fees so as to result in the lowest cost to the user, consistent with the user's policy constraints.

In Ancama's case, the basic objective function is as follows:

MINIMIZE 0.016667 TOBAL + 0.016667 TORCV + TOFEE - 0.00001 HQHQD - 0.00001 HQTAX
where

TOBAL   = the sum of average company cash ledger balances

TORCV   = the average investment that the company has in retail lock-box receivables that have been mailed by customers but have not yet been received by a lock-box bank and recorded on the company's books[4]

---

[4] TORCV is a constant in the first four CASH ALPHA runs, because the mailing pattern from customers to lock-boxes does not change. However, TORCV becomes an independent variable in the final CASH ALPHA run, the test of a new lock-box location, and so it is important to include TORCV in the earlier cases for comparative purposes.

TOFEE   = the sum of cash fees that the company pays

HQHQD   = unallocated disbursements made by headquarters, which are explained later

HQTAX   = unallocated tax payments, also explained later

(A listing of mnemonic symbols used in CASH ALPHA for Ancama is included as Appendix G.)

The 0.016667 coefficient is the monthly equivalent of an annual pretax cost of capital of 20 per cent (.20/12 = .016667). The 0.00001 coefficient applied to HQHQD and HQTAX is an artifice used to segregate any leftover headquarters disbursements or tax payments. It should be noted that all other tax payments, and float created by disbursing, bear a zero cost to the company, as reflected in the objective function. Were it not for the very small artificial credit of .001 per cent per month on these leftover disbursements and taxes, the computer would not segregate them for allocation by company financial management. Rather, it would simply dump leftover items in the most convenient bank.

The company's objective function can be restated as follows: we shall try to minimize the monthly cost of maintaining the company's banking system on the assumption that float and tax payments have a zero cost to the company but that investment reflected in average ledger balances carries an opportunity cost of 20 per cent per year pretax to the company.

2.10 Equations for the National Bank of Chicago

The National Bank of Chicago is Ancama's bench-mark bank in that Ancama uses it to measure the service-charge/credit terms of other banks. This is not to say that Ancama attempts to hold other banks to the National Bank of Chicago basis. But it does find that the latter provides a convenient measuring device.

In describing its relationship with this bank, Ancama's financial management settled on the following equations: (See Appendix G for a definition of the abbreviations used. Also see Appendix H for a listing of *all* equations used in the Ancama examples.)

a. CHCST = 0.02 CHCXD + 0.05 CHCXP + CHMUC - CHMUK + CHOMC + 0.0375 CHRLB + 0.065 CHWLB

This equation describes the bank's price schedule as it applies to Ancama. Total cost (CHCST) equals 2¢ for every check deposited (0.02 CHCXD) plus 5¢ for every check paid (0.05 CHCXP) plus "makeup" costs (CHMUC) minus negative "makeup" costs (CHMUK) plus other monthly costs (CHOMC) plus 3.75¢ for every retail lock-box item (0.0375 CHRLB) plus 6.5¢ for every wholesale lock-box item (0.065 CHWLB). "Makeup" costs (CHMUC and

CHMUK) result from inexactness in predicting, and is explained in some detail later. CASH ALPHA's use as a monthly planner for determining where to disburse, where to make tax payments, and where to pay fees is dependent on accurate predictions of "inputs" such as the number of retail lock-box items that will be processed during any given month at any given bank. Small predicting errors are to be expected. In the case of a bank that has a fee agreement with Ancama, these small errors will normally result in slightly different fees than predicted. But in the case of banks that are compensated wholly by a combination of balances and/or tax payments, there will be analysis overages and shortfalls. The "MUC" category reflects a compensation shortfall that has been carried over from a prior month. For example, earnings credit on balances and tax payments might have fallen $40 below the bank's total service charge for September, in which case CASH ALPHA would attempt to establish compensation in October at a level sufficient to pay for October services plus the $40 shortfall. The "MUK" is the opposite of a shortfall; it is an overage, which CASH ALPHA uses to reduce the level of predicted compensation during the following month. The figure for any one month's calculation is implicitly a cumulative total of MUC and MUK from inception of the system.

Other monthly costs, "OMC," include a variety of charges that are simply too small or too steady to warrant individual equations or predictions. In the case of the National Bank of Chicago, OMC during a typical month includes $30 of wire transfer charges, $25 for account reconciliation, and $35 for postage.

  b. CHCTN = 0.05063 CHDEP

This equation states that checks in transit (CTN) are a function of deposits, and averages .05063 times the total deposits in a given month. Thus if deposits for a month totaled $5,000,000, checks in transit (based on our normal experience) for the month, on average, would be (0.05063) ($5,000,000) or $253,000. A more elaborate CTN calculation is explained later.

  c. CHCXD = 0.0007

This is the first of the prediction equations. The accounting center estimates that approximately 700 checks will be deposited in this bank during a normal month in addition to RLB and WLB items. Independent variables are written in the Ancama example in millions. Thus 1.2 would be 1,200,000 and .0007 would be 700.

  d. CHCXP = 0.000517 CHDIS

This describes a historical relationship between the number of checks paid (CXP) and the number of dollars disbursed (DIS). If, for example, disbursements on CA (Chicago Accounting Center) totaled $5,000,000 in a given month, experience indicates that this would mean about (0.000517) ($5,000,000) or 2,585 checks. This is another way of saying that checks disbursed on CH average $1/0.000517 or about $1,934. In any given month the average check written will vary to some extent. Errors caused by departures from this historical average will be made up through the makeup cost (MUC and MUK) mechanism. Note that the coefficient is based on accounting center experience, not on individual bank experience.

  e. CHDEP = 7.328

This is a prediction by the accounting center. It says that in a normal month $3,078,000 is received in retail lock-box remittances, $4,000,000 in wholesale lock-box remittances, and $250,000 in other receipts that are deposited in CH, for a total of $7,328,000.

  f. CHFEE ⩽ 1/3 CHTVL

This equation describes a limitation on the use of fees that the bank insisted on. It says that the total fee paid (FEE) may be equal to or less than one-third the total of compensation received by the bank. Restated, it means that at least two-thirds of compensation to this bank must take the form of service-charge credit on balances or on tax payments.

  g. CHLNS = 0.35

This equation describes loans outstanding. For input into CASH ALPHA, Ancama uses a simple six-month moving average, and during the past six months average loans outstanding (LNS) have totaled $350,000.

  h. CHMUC - CHMUK = 0.0

During the normal month (as calculated at inception of the use of CASH ALPHA) there are no makeup costs (MUC) or makeup credits (MUK). Had there been a shortfall of $50 from the prior month the right-hand side would have been 0.00005 and not zero. An overage of $50 would be reflected by a right-hand side of - 0.00005.[5]

---

[5] Since variables in linear programming cannot take on negative values, any variable that can be either positive or negative must be represented by two variables: the positive part and the negative part. All the coefficients of the negative variable are multiplied by -1, so that when the actual variable takes on a negative value, the corresponding linear programming variable takes on a positive value. This is shown graphically, as follows:

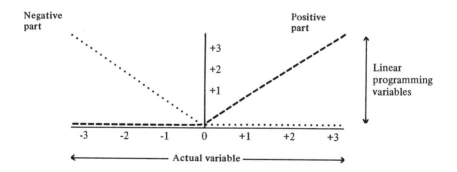

Thus, actual = "positive part" - "negative part."

i. CHNCB = CHBAL + 0.19459 CHDIS - CHCTN

This equation describes average net collected balances (NCB) during the month. To approximate float generated by disbursements, we apply a co-efficient of 0.19459 to disbursements made on this bank. By this we mean that, on average, a dollar of disbursements made on CH during a normal month generates average monthly balances of 19.459¢. Thus, our total NCB at CH during any given month is equal to average company cash book balances (BAL) plus a function of disbursements (0.19459 CHDIS) less the in-transit on deposits at CH that has been calculated. The shortcomings of this predicting equation are described later.

j. CHOMC = 0.00009

Other monthly costs (OMC) equal $90. This is an aggregation of those charges that vary little from month to month.

k. CHRCV = 0.494054

This equation states that the company's average investment in retail lock-box receivables that have been mailed by customers but have not yet been received by a lock-box bank and made available for recording on the company's books is $494,054. This equation, and the expanded version of it explained later, become important when CASH ALPHA is used in heuristic testing of the addition of a new lock-box bank. I assume that receipt of items by a lock-box bank and the capability of posting customers' ledgers to reflect receipt of these checks occur on the same day, which should be possible with wire transmission of taped data from a bank's computer center to the company's computer center.

l. CHRLB = 0.073

This equation states that 73,000 retail lock-box items flow through the CH retail lock-box in a normal month. A new number would be predicted each month, which would take into account seasonal as well as long-term change factors.

m. CHTVL = CHFEE + CHVNB + CHVTP

This equation states that the total value of compensation received by the bank (TVL) equals the sum of fees paid to the bank (FEE) plus the value of net collected balances to the bank (VNB) plus the value of tax payments to the bank (VTP).

n. CHVNB = 0.003566 CHNCB

The bank agreed to give service-charge credit on "available for investment" balances on the basis of the rate it was paying on 180-day C.D.'s. At the time of the initial CASH ALPHA calculations this rate was 5 1/8 per cent. Thus the monthly coefficient to be applied to net collected balances was the earnings rate times the percentage of balances available for investment after reserve requirements times the number of days in the month divided by the number

of days in the year used in calculating service-charge credit. This is calculated
as follows:

$$(0.05125)(0.835)(30/360) = 0.003566$$

Thus average balances of $1,000,000 during a month would generate a
service-charge credit of $(0.003566)($1,000,000)$ or $3,566.00. The coefficient
in this equation needs to be updated each time the program is run to reflect
the current C.D. rate.

    o. CHVTP = 0.00203 CHTAX

The bank agreed to give service-charge credit on the after-reserve balances
created by tax payments on the basis of a fourth of 1 per cent below the
Federal Funds rate as of the first day of the month, on the assumption that
the bank would have twenty days' use of the funds. The monthly coefficient
was calculated for the first month of use by multiplying the earnings rate (the
then Federal Funds rate of 4 5/8 per cent - 1/4 per cent, or 4 3/8 per cent) times
the number of days that it was assumed the bank would have the funds divided
by the number of days in the year used to calculate service-charge credit.
The calculation is as follows:

$$(0.04375)(0.835)(20/360) = 0.00203$$

Thus $1,000,000 in tax payments would generate $2,030.00 of service-charge
credits. This equation also needs updating each time CASH ALPHA is run.

    p. CHWLB = 0.0051

This equation reflects the accounting center's prediction that 5,100 wholesale lock-box items will be processed during the normal month. Like RLB,
WLB is predicted by the accounting center each time CASH ALPHA is run.

    q. CHCST $\leqslant$ CHTVL

This equation requires that predicted total value given to CH (TVL) be
equal or greater than predicted total cost of services provided by the bank to
the company (CST).

    r. CHNCB $\geqslant$ 0.15 CHLNS + 0.5

This equation sets a minimum balance level. The equation states that
NCB shall be at least equal to or greater than the sum of 15 per cent of average
loans outstanding over the past six months (LNS) plus $500,000, which the
company feels will give it a call on $5,000,000 of additional loans at this
bank.

    s. CHVTP $\leqslant$ 1/3 CHTVL

This equation represents another bank requirement. The bank is willing
to take tax payments as compensation for services performed, but it will not
take payment beyond one-third of the total value of compensation for services
to be received each month by the bank.

The following equations deal with several banks. They have a direct bearing
on allocation of business to CH during any month:

t. TOTAX: 3BTAX + CHTAX + HQTAX + LSTAX + PTTAX + USTAX + WTTAX = 4.003

This equation describes the payment of all taxes ($4,003,000) by Ancama during the month. It does not say *how* they will be allocated — CASH ALPHA will compute this.

u. CADIS: 2DDIS + 2YDIS + CHDIS + LSDIS = 9.6

This equation states that all general disbursements made by the Chicago Accounting Center (CADIS) of $9,600,000 will be made on four banks, the three major regional banks — the National Bank of Chicago (CH), La Salle Street Trust Company (LS), and the Second National Bank of Dallas (2D) — and also on the Second National Bank of New York (2Y). As the objective function calls for the minimization of costs within the entire Ancama system, we can expect the Chicago Accounting Center to shunt disbursements to the Second National Bank of New York when it is more profitable for the system as a whole to use fees and tax payments locally and to use float to reduce company cash ledger balances in those banks where large balances are maintained as a call on credit, such as the New York banks.

If we were trying to minimize costs by *accounting center,* then balances created by float above constraint minimums might be used to eliminate fees rather than to displace book balances at the major New York banks, but this may be uneconomic for the system as a whole. Each of Ancama's accounting centers is linked with one New York bank, in the sense that each center draws on a separate New York bank when it does disburse on New York. A separate account is maintained with these New York banks for use by the accounting center.

On what basis will CASH ALPHA allocate disbursements? It will normally disburse where it can obtain the greatest float. In the case of CH, the float coefficient is 0.19459; for LS it is 0.20377; for 2D it is 0.22593. Among these three banks, CASH ALPHA will allocate float to 2D until the minimum NCB needed at 2D are met. Then CASH ALPHA will move on to the next highest generator of float. In Ancama's case, management decided to assign to the New York banks a coefficient (for regional accounting center disbursements) equal to the average of the float coefficients at the other accounting center banks rather than one equal to what experience showed could be generated if it disbursed from an accounting center city on a New York bank. It simply did not want to do what it felt might be "overplaying" the use of float, subjectively determined. A similar end result could have been achieved by placing constraints on minimum disbursements at any one or any group of banks.

Ancama's arbitrary method of calculating float on the New York banks will normally underestimate float at these banks. Because the level of service charges does not determine the level of business with the New York banks (average NCB do) it is necessary to have an out-of-system control on the administration of these three vital accounts. This would be relatively simple. Book balances could be adjusted weekly or daily to bring NCB into line with predetermined balance levels. In lieu of weekly or daily adjustments, Ancama could simply target NCB at a higher level following a shortfall, and vice versa.

3 THE ANCAMA CORPORATION CASES

Five CASH ALPHA cases were run in one session on an IBM 7094 computer, utilizing LP/94, a general linear programming model developed by C-E-I-R, Inc. Appendix H lists the equations used in the five cases. Because the five cases were run at one time, the equation listing is somewhat more complex than would be necessary in an ongoing system. Appendix I is a reproduction of portions of the computer printout for one of the cases.

As noted earlier, Ancama Corporation is a mythical company created to demonstrate CASH ALPHA. Its banks are equally mythical. Thus the "discussions" and "negotiations" in this chapter are simply fictional accounts that add, I hope, some degree of realism to a wholly mythical case study.

3.1. The Base Case

The solution printout of the base case[1] (Appendix I) shows the optimal selection of independent variables. In summary they are shown in Table 3.1.

---

[1] The "base case" is the first computer solution, *not* the pre-CASH ALPHA case.

Table 3.1.   Allocation of Variables in the Base Case

Tax Payments

3BTAX	$ 398,800.43
CHTAX	523,411.89
PTTAX	584,836.62
USTAX	708,963.82
WTTAX	208,260.54
HQTAX	1,578,727.01 (unallocated)
TOTAX	$4,003,000.00

Cash Fees

CHFEE	$154.84
USFEE	172.01
TOFEE	$326.85

Headquarters Disbursements

2YHQD	$10,255,000.00
MNHQD	1,465,000.00
WSHQD	2,930,000.00
HQHQD	–
NYHQD	$14,650,000.00

Boston Accounting Center Disbursements

3BDIS	–
MNDIS	$1,472,903.05
PTDIS	417,096.95
BADIS	$1,890,000.00

Chicago Accounting Center Disbursements

2DDIS	$4,299,647.79
2YDIS	3,538,709.09
CHDIS	564,084.74
LSDIS	1,197,558.37
CADIS	$9,600,000.00

San Francisco Accounting Center Disbursements

USDIS	$2,429,264.33
UTDIS	–
WSDIS	3,380,735.67
SFDIS	$5,810,000.00

The total monthly cost of this solution, in comparison with the pre-CASH ALPHA case, is shown in Table 3.2. On a 6 per cent cost-of-money basis, instead of the 20 per cent opportunity cost used in Tables 3.1 and 3.2, the figures show a considerable saving although one that is much less dramatic. Table 3.3 illustrates this.

Table 3.2. Comparison of Cost Before and After CASH ALPHA Base Case –
20 per cent Pretax Opportunity Cost

	Pre-CASH ALPHA	CASH ALPHA Base Case	Savings over Pre-CASH ALPHA
TOBAL at 20 per cent	$168,070.03	$115,608.22	$52,461.81
TORCV at 20 per cent	8,234.40	8,234.40	–
TOFEE	–	326.85	(326.85)
Subtotal	$176,304.43	$124,169.47	$52,134.96
Less HQTAX credit	–	15.78	(15.78)
Solution cost	$176,304.43	$124,153.69	$52,150.74

Table 3.3. Comparison of Cost Before and After CASH ALPHA
Base Case – 6 per cent Pretax Opportunity Cost

	Pre-CASH ALPHA	CASH ALPHA Base Case	Savings over Pre-CASH ALPHA
TOBAL at 6 per cent	$50,420.00	$34,681.77	$15,738.23
TORCV at 6 per cent	2,470.27	2,470.27	–
TOFEE	–	326.85	(326.85)
Subtotal	$52,890.27	$37,478.89	$15,411.38
Less HQTAX credit	–	15.78	(15.78)
Solution cost	$52,890.27	$37,463.11	$15,427.16

(Similar detail for other CASH ALPHA cases, is shown in Appendix D.)
These savings result mainly from reduced average balances. A comparison
of company cash ledger balances and net collected balances on a before-and-
after basis are given in Tables 3.4 and 3.5.

Table 3.4. Comparison of Company Ledger Balances Before and After
CASH ALPHA Base Case

	Pre-CASH ALPHA	CASH ALPHA Base Case	Savings over Pre-CASH ALPHA
2Y	$2,300,000.00	–	$2,300,000.00
WS	3,785,000.00	$3,284,976.88	500,023.12
MN	1,000,000.00	1,195,814.16	(195,814.16)
CH	503,000.00	813,751.39	(310,751.39)
LS	100,000.00	–	100,000.00
3S	250,000.00	250,000.00	–
2D	345,000.00	–	345,000.00
3B	946,000.00	562,301.91	383,698.09
WT	150,000.00	45,164.18	104,835.82
PT	271,000.00	–	271,000.00
ES	150,000.00	150,000.00	–
US	–	–	–
UT	184,000.00	534,346.16	(350,346.16)
LA	–	–	–
SV	100,000.00	100,000.00	–
Total	$10,084,000.00	$6,936,354.69	$3,147,645.31

**Table 3.5. Comparison of Net Collected Balances Before and After
CASH ALPHA Base Case**

	Pre-CASH ALPHA	CASH ALPHA Base Case	Savings over Pre-CASH ALPHA
2Y	$3,160,000.00	$3,100,000.00	$60,000.00
WS	4,197,000.00	4,000,000.00	197,000.00
MN	2,150,000.00	1,757,500.00	392,500.00
CH	959,000.00	552,500.00	406,500.00
LS	948,000.00	552,500.00	395,500.00
3S	250,000.00	250,000.00	–
2D	849,000.00	866,616.79	(17,616.79)
3B	1,125,000.00	500,000.00	625,000.00
WT	209,000.00	104,170.18	104,829.82
PT	325,000.00	26,329.94	298,670.06
ES	150,000.00	150,000.00	–
US	616,000.00	500,000.00	116,000.00
UT	350,000.00	350,000.00	–
LA	267,000.00	–	267,000.00
SV	100,000.00	100,000.00	–
Total	$15,655,000.00	$12,809,616.91	$2,845,383.09

It can be misleading to focus on company ledger balances. For example,
as much as $2,300,000.00 of ledger balances was cut from the Second
National Bank of New York. But in terms of net collected balances at this
bank, the cut was only $60,000, from $3,160,000 to $3,100,000. What
this meant, of course, was that if it followed the CASH ALPHA base case,
Ancama would disburse considerably more on this bank than it ever had
before. Instead of the normal $3,150,000 of headquarters disbursements
on this bank plus the dividend payments (which average $2,250,000 per
quarter or $750,000 per month), Ancama would disburse $10,255,000 of
its headquarters payments and $3,538,709.09 of the Chicago Accounting
Center payments on this bank, in addition to the dividend payments. As a
result the bank itself would continue to receive about the same net collected
balances that it had prior to the CASH ALPHA base case — the $60,000
difference would be a policy trimming of this relationship. Charges would
go up because of added volume, but this would still be trivial in relationship
to the value of the business to the bank. Based on the CH charge structure
(Ancama does not request an analysis statement from 2Y) the 2Y relationship
shows value of NCB at $11,054.60 but costs of only $990.98.

Savings over pre-CASH ALPHA are greater by about $300,000 in terms of
company ledger balances than in terms of net collected balances. The major
reason for this is that CASH ALPHA is influenced by the float that can be
generated by drawing on more distant banks. Of the $9,600,000 disbursed
by the Chicago Accounting Center, only about $1,762,000 is disbursed on
the two Chicago banks — the balance is disbursed on New York and Dallas

banks. Two qualifying points are important here. First, the coefficients used in this example probably reflect wider dispersion than a careful analysis of a "real world" situation would disclose. Second, the setting of constraints here is an important area for policy decision. Despite the value that a company can obtain by generating increased float, it will probably want to put limits on its use of float. A reasonable limit would probably be for a regional disbursing center to disburse on regional banks, or on New York or Chicago banks, or on the company's headquarters-town banks. To illustrate this last point, it seems reasonable to me for the Los Angeles office of a Cleveland-based firm to pay on a Cleveland bank, but it would *not* be reasonable for a Los Angeles office of a New York-based firm to pay on a Cleveland bank.

The largest single source of savings in this first test of CASH ALPHA comes from use of the firm's tax payments to compensate banks for tangible services performed. Diversion of these payments adversely affects Ancama's New York banks. However, analysis of their position shows that the business that is left with these banks compensates them for both the tangible and intangible services that are valuable to Ancama. For example, at Wall Street Trust — Ancama's major international bank — the value of net collected balances (on the CH credit/charge basis) in the CASH ALPHA base case is $14,264.00, and the cost of tangible services performed is $269.28. Ancama calculates that the value of intangible services sought by Ancama is about $84,000 per year, or $7,000 per month. Thus there is still a considerable sum on deposit that is paying for neither tangibles nor intangibles, except that it is performing the vital function of acting as a call on borrowed money. The bank suffers *in comparison with what it had before* but not in terms of the services that Ancama seeks.

Even with the increased use of tax payments to compensate the banks for tangible services performed, the HQTAX category of unallocated tax payments totals $1,578,727.01. This means that the constraints set by various banks (such as CH's requirement that tax payments provide no more than one-third of total compensation) limit additional use of tax payments to pay for tangible services. At this point Ancama might simply allocate the HQTAX among the three New York banks, as it historically allocated them, or it might select some other nonquantified basis for distribution. At the same time, the existence of these left-over tax payments within the system gives rise to strong incentive for structural change of the system so as to take advantage of them.

Before considering structural change, it may be of value to analyze the base case solution as it affects one bank, our "bench-mark" National Bank of Chicago.

Table 3.6.   Analysis of CH in the Base Case

Activity	Thousands of Items	Thousands of Dollars	Marginal Costs Dollars per Item	Marginal Costs Dollars per Dollar Charge	Charge Dollars per Item
Checks paid	.3		.0333		.05
Checks deposited	.7		.01333		.02
Retail lock-box	73.0		.025		.0375
Wholesale lock-box	5.1		.0433		.065
Checks in transit		371.0		.0167	
Loans		350.0		.002	

	Thousands of Dollars	Credits	Charges	Marginal Value Dollars per Dollar Charge
Total Charges			$3,187.58	- .668
Average NCB	552.5			.0167
Credit value		$1,970.21		1.0
Tax payments	523.4			.000
Credit value		1,062.53		1.0
Fee		154.84		1.0
Total credits			$3,187.58	

3.2.   The National Bank of Chicago in the Base Case

An analysis of the base case for CH is shown in Table 3.6. The computer prints out not only the optimal solution but also the marginal costs, or "shadow prices," of each item in solution. Note, for example, that all of the marginal costs for routine activity items are precisely two-thirds of the stated charge per item. For example, the bank charges 5¢ per check paid, but the computer calculates that the marginal cost for one more such item is only 3.33¢. The reason for this becomes clear when we look at the lower portion of Table 3.6. The solution calls for tax payments of $523,411.89 to CH. This results in an earnings credit of $1,062.53, which is just one-third of the total charge of $3,187.58. When the bank agreed to take tax payments and allow service-charge credit on them, it stipulated that tax payments would provide credit for no more than one-third of total charges. Thus we see an example of taxes being "constrained out" here because we have reached the limit of our use of tax payments for the current level of business done with this bank. But this also means that an additional check paid through CH would cost Ancama 3.33¢, not 5¢, because it could compensate the bank for one-third of the total charge with tax payments. Because Ancama has unused tax payments (HQTAX), there is no implicit cost in diverting additional tax payments to CH. Even if all tax payments were used to pay for tangible services, it might be advantageous to shift some to CH, but there would then be a cost to such a shift because additional balances or fees would be needed elsewhere to pay for the services that had been paid for by the tax payments shifted to CH.

Willingness to give service-charge credit for tax payments could be very important in giving one bank a competitive advantage over another. Consider, for example, the situation in which two banks in the same city are seeking the wholesale lock-box of a common customer, Firm Y. Both allow the same service-charge credit on balances. Both charge 6.5¢ per item and accept fees as well as balances to pay for services. But Bank A does not give service-charge credit on tax payments, whereas Bank B does. From the company's standpoint, the *marginal* cost to the company of using Bank B might be 4.33¢, if Bank B agreed to take up to one-third of total compensation in the form of tax payments (as did CH; note the marginal cost of wholesale lock-box items in Table 3.6) *and* if the company had tax payments that were unallocated and available to pay for such a service. Beyond this, Bank B would be more competitive *as far as a company with "excess" tax payments is concerned*, with a 7.5¢ per-item charge (a marginal cost to the company of 5¢) than would Bank A with a charge of 6.5¢ per item!

Carrying this example further, consider the competitive advantage of the bank that accepts balances, tax payments, and fees over the bank that accepts only balances in compensation for services performed. Assume that there is a third bank competing with Banks A and B for the wholesale lock-box. Bank C quotes a 6.5¢ per-item charge, but it does not give service-charge credit on tax payments and it does not want to do business on a fee basis. The only way a firm can "pay" for the service is with deposit balances. Assume that Bank C allows 3 per cent per annum, or 0.25 per cent per month, on net collected balances. The company must have $26.00 on deposit on average over the month to pay for each wholesale lock-box item (.0025 times $26.00 = 6.5¢). If, prior to consideration of this new lock-box, Firm Y had sufficient liquidity through credit-line support and additional calls on credit, then the decision to do business with Bank C rather than with Bank A or Bank B would involve an incremental investment in cash of $26.00 per wholesale lock-box item that would flow through this bank during the month. The opportunity cost of this $26.00 will in all liklihood be in excess of the 3 per cent per annum service-charge allowance provided by the bank. If Firm Y calculated its capital cost at Ancama's level, or 1.6667 per cent per month before taxes, then the marginal cost of processing one item is the firm's opportunity rate times the required investment per item processed. In this case the marginal cost would be

$$(0.016667)(\$26.00) = \$0.433$$

Assuming that Firm Y is not engaged in capital rationing, and that it calculates its opportunity cost at a current money rate, for example, 5.125 per cent per year or 0.4271 per cent per month, then the marginal cost would be

$$(0.004271)(\$26.00) = \$0.111$$

Thus, although all three banks quote a 6.5¢ per-item charge, the marginal cost to Firm Y varies widely, depending on its current status with respect to tax payments and capital rationing, as shown in Table 3.7. Again, it is not important to belabor the cost-of-capital point to see the issue illustrated here. It is apparent that what is of value to the company is the *flexibility* to utilize cash fees and tax payments in lieu of deposit balances.

Table 3.7. Marginal Cost of WLB Process for Firm Y

With Bank A or Bank B – fee basis	6.50¢
With Bank B, using tax payments and cash fee, assuming that Firm Y currently has "excess" tax payments	4.33¢
With Bank C, assuming capital rationing, and thus a 20 per cent pretax opportunity rate	43.33¢
With Bank C, assuming no capital rationing, and thus a 5.125 per cent pretax opportunity rate	11.10¢

Returning to the analysis of the National Bank of Chicago in Table 3.6, there is a marginal cost of $0.0167 per month for each $1.00 of checks in transit. This means only that any decrease in CTN can be reinvested by the firm at its pretax opportunity rate of 20 per cent per year. The next item, a marginal cost of $0.002 per month per $1.00 of loans outstanding is a bit more complicated. If Ancama reduced average loans at CH by $1.00, then balances could go down by 15 per cent of that, or 15¢, while still conforming to the constraint that describes compensating balances. If balances were reduced by 15¢, then the company could reinvest this amount at its opportunity rate of 1.6667 per cent per month, for earnings of ($0.15)(0.016667) or $0.0025 per month. But by withdrawing the 15¢ from the bank, fees would have to go up at CH to pay for the earnings credit that was earned by the 15¢ of balances, which was 0.003566 CHNCB, or (0.003566)($0.15), or $0.0005. Thus the net savings to Ancama of a reduction of $1.00 in loans outstanding is $0.0025 - $0.0005, or 2¢ per $1.00 per month. This figure could be highly useful to the firm in determining the best place to do its line borrowing or the best syndication for a term loan.

Looking again at the bottom section of Table 3.6, we see that average NCB are $552,500. The reason for this, of course, is to provide the 15 per cent compensating balance level on the $350,000 of average loans outstanding, or $52,500 plus the $500,000 call on credit. Since this constraint exists, and since we assumed the ability to make dual use of balances for both activity charge and compensating balance/credit call requirements, CASH ALPHA calculates the service-charge value of these funds that the constraint says *must* be at CH, then CASH ALPHA "fills up" on tax payments until constrained out at one-third of the total compensation level, and finally selects the payment of fees for whatever is left over.

The marginal value column of the lower section of Table 3.6. illustrates CASH ALPHA's preference for tax payments for additional compensation to the banks. Tax payments carry an incremental cost of zero, compared with an incremental cost of $0.0167, or 1.6667 per cent per month, on net collected balances, and with an incremental cost of cash fees equal to the fees that would be payable.

It might be useful to know what one item of a variable *not* included in the optimal solution would do to total solution cost. The "D/J" or "delta-j" provided by the computer gives us this information for the base case (Appendix J). For example, in the base case 2DBAL is zero — all NCB at 2D are the result of float generated by disbursement activity. If, arbitrarily, we inserted $1.00 of 2DBAL into the solution, then disbursements could be diverted from 2D to another bank, where, however, a dollar of DIS results in lower NCB than at 2D. This shift of DIS away from 2D would also mean a very slight decrease in cost at 2D, because lower disbursements would mean lower CXP costs, and this in turn would allow a further decrease in disbursements at 2D. But if DIS are shifted out of 2D, then costs at other banks will go up to reflect additional CXP costs at those banks. The net effect on total solution cost of all changes required to satisfy all constraints when introducing $1.00 of 2DBAL is the delta-j figure for 2DBAL, or 0.00156045, or about 0.156¢.

3.3.   Individual Bank Optimization versus System Optimization

The importance of the systems approach over individual component optimization can perhaps best be shown by an example. The base case solution for Ancama's major West Coast bank, the U.S. National Bank of California (US), calls for a combination of net collected balances, tax payments, and fees as shown in Table 3.8.

Table 3.8.   Compensation of US in Base Case

	Thousands of Dollars	Credits	Charges
Total Charges			$2,220.48
Average NCB	500.0		
Credit value		$1,348.00	
Tax payments	709.0		
Credit value		$ 740.16	
Subtotal – Credit value			$2,088.16
Service-charge shortfall			$ 132.32
Cash Fee – 130 per cent of service-charge shortfall			$ 172.01

Less than half of the San Francisco Accounting Center's disbursements are made on US. The balance of disbursements is scheduled for WS, the Wall Street Trust Company. Only sufficient disbursements to give NCB of $500,000 are scheduled for US. The composition of NCB at US is given in Table 3.9.

Table 3.9. Composition of NCB at US in Base Case

USBAL	
+0.26017 USDIS = (0.26017)($2,429,264.33) =	$632,021.69
+0.0775 USPAY = (0.0775)($1,200,000.00) =	93,000.00
Subtotal − Gross average bank ledger balances =	$725,021.69
−USCTN: USCTN = 0.046685 USDEP = (0.046685)($4,820,000) =	225,021.69
USNCB	$500,000.00

It would certainly be possible to keep some additional disbursements in the San Francisco area. By making additional disbursements on US, fees there would be reduced. But this is uneconomic, as we shall see. For example, Ancama could divert $188,646.30 from WS to US. This would increase USNCB by (0.26017)($188,646.30) or $49,080.11, which in turn would generate additional service-charge credit of $132.32, sufficient to eliminate the service-charge shortfall and thus to save the cash fee of $172.01 (the arrangement with US calls for cash fees at 130 per cent of service-charge shortfall).

But if we divert $188,646.30 of disbursements from WS, we shall reduce NCB at WS by (0.25476)($188,646.30) or $48,059.53. Another WS constraint calls for NCB there to be 15 per cent of average line usage plus 10 per cent of average unused lines plus $1,000,000, and as balances at WS were just meeting this constraint, the loss of disbursements to US necessitates additional ledger balances of $48,059.53 at WS. At the capital cost of 1.6667 per cent per month assigned to book balances, this added investment in cash at WS costs $801.01, far more than the savings of $172.01 at US. A switch in disbursements from WS to US would make sense only if the Ancama opportunity cost fell to $172.01/$48,059.53 per month, or 0.3579 per cent per month, or 4.29 per cent per year before taxes. As is stated earlier, my own feeling is that a firm's banking structure should be designed so as to minimize cost measured on a cost-of-capital basis. But in a period of transition, CASH ALPHA could prove useful in making possible a periodic analysis of the advantages of investing a portion of short-term portfolio funds in cash balances to eliminate cash fees.[2]

---

[2] An unpublished doctoral dissertation entitled "Cash Budgeting, the Payments Schedule, and Short-Term Financing by Business Firms," by Yair E. Orgler, Carnegie Institute of Technology, appears to have interesting integration possibilities with CASH ALPHA.

3.4. Excessive Float

What does the firm do if its generation of float provides net collected balances at its banks well in excess of equitable compensation to the banks for tangible and intangible services? In the Ancama base case, CASH ALPHA simply shunted excessive float to major credit reservoir banks, and the excessive float then eliminated the need for company book balances at these major banks. An alternate mechanism, if there are no major book balances to displace, would be to pay a category of disbursements by draft instead of by check.

3.5. Amending the Base Case

Based on the zero marginal cost of tax payments, Ancama's next step was to change the structure of compensation within the system so as to make more effective use of tax payments.

Ancama maintained relatively large but essentially dormant accounts with banks in three plant towns. In each case there was a $25,000 plant manager's "emergency" account, and in addition a dormant demand deposit account ranging in size from $75,000 to $225,000. Ancama decided to replace a portion of the dormant balance with each of these banks with tax payments on a two-for-one basis. For example, Ancama planned to reduce the balance in the regular account at the Third National Bank of South Bend from $225,000 to $125,000, but at the same time it would make monthly tax payments of $200,000 through the bank, which would leave the bank with the same level of total average demand deposits, assuming a fifteen-day average retention period for tax payments. The two-for-one ratio would have to be adjusted periodically to reflect trends in the number of days that tax payments would be used by the banks. In similar fashion, Ancama planned to replace $50,000 in demand deposits with $100,000 per month in tax payments at each of Ancama's other plant banks (Elm Street Trust and Sunnyville Trust).

Ancama also modified its relationships with Union Trust Company to take advantage of its excess tax payments. Union Trust was helpful to Ancama in providing particularly valuable information on real-estate activities in Southern California, a key growth market for Ancama's retail operation. Union Trust's major tangible service for Ancama was the wholesale lock-box. A little over 60 per cent of the wholesale lock-box volume flowed through Union Trust, with the balance processed by U.S. National. Ancama had, as a matter of policy, kept net collected balances of $350,000 with Union Trust, which gave that bank monthly profits of $420.15 in excess of the profit implicit in the bank's unfavorable charge/credit rate structure. The monthly relationship, based on the UT charge/credit formula and on the CH basis, is shown in Table 3.10.

Table 3.10. Summary of UT Charge/Credit Formula Values

	UT Basis	CH Basis
Value of NCB (VNB)	$791.70	$1,248.10
Less activity charges (CST)	371.55	371.55
Excess of VNB over CST	$420.15	$ 876.55

Ancama felt that the value of the real-estate advisory service provided by UT was worth $10,000 per year to it, or roughly $833 per month, although the matter of valuation of this service had never been discussed with the bank. Even though Union Trust's analysis statement reflected only $420.15 of excessive NCB value, this did not place Ancama in a dilemma. Ancama reasoned that it had calculated the value of the intangible service on the basis of what it would have paid in the form of fees for that service. Accordingly, it reasoned that fair compensation should be based on the slate of charges/ credits of a major bank that was willing to perform such services on its charge/credit slate basis and not on the basis of a charge/credit structure that significantly understated the value of compensation (in the form of average balances) to the bank.

Ancama could have reasoned that, because of Union Trust's comparatively low rate of credit on balances, Ancama should set a correspondingly low value on the real-estate advisory service, and the results would have been much the same. The calculation of the value of such an intangible service to a company is sufficiently subjective so that a wide variety of policy positions could be taken by a number of companies, all seeking to compensate their banks for essentially the same services.

The company discussed the possibility of replacing $150,000 of the average net collected balances at the bank with $300,000 of tax payments monthly. This would leave NCB at UT at the level of $200,000. The bank raised no objection to this procedure but asked that Ancama keep in mind the fluctuations in the number of days' usage of tax payments.

Although Ancama did not seek a service-charge credit value from Union Trust on tax payments, and the bank did not suggest one, Ancama recomputed monthly profits on the new terms, as shown in Table 3.11. The profitability

Table 3.11. Summary of UT Charge/Credit Formula Values with Tax Payments

	UT Basis	CH Basis
Value of NCB (VNB)	$452.40	$713.20
Value of TAX	(not quantified)	609.00
Total value (TVL)	$452.40+	$1,422.20
Less activity charges (CST)	371.55	371.55
Excess of TVL over CST	$80.85+	$1,050.65

of this relationship is increased on the CH basis, which assumes that taxes will average twenty days' availability.

The net result of changes at these four banks is to reduce both average book balances and average net collected balances by $350,000, while reducing the pool of unallocated tax payments by $700,000 per month. Total solution cost drops by $5,826.45 per month from $124,153.69 to $118,327.24. (See Appendix D for a summary of all changes from the base case.) The figure of $5,826.45 results from the application of Ancama's opportunity cost of 1.6667 per cent per month to the $350,000 of reduced investment, to get (0.016667)($350,000) or $5,833.45 (the "real" savings) less the artificial 0.001 per cent per month value of unallocated tax payments, or (0.00001)($700,000) or $7.00, for a net solution savings of $5,826.45. At a 6 per cent opportunity cost factor, and leaving aside the artificial tax cost, the savings are worth (0.005)($350,000) or $1,750 per month.

3.6. A Reduced Call on Credit

As the CASH ALPHA study progressed, it became apparent to Ancama's financial management that the company still had far more borrowing potential to finance a major investment opportunity than it had set as its objective. On a strictly mechanical basis, it calculated its call on credit at $84.6 million, as demonstrated in Table 3.12. Ancama had originally project-

Table 3.12. Calculation of Call on Credit Based on Base Case
              (thousands of dollars)

Bank	NCB	NCB Supporting Loans and Lines	"Uncommitted" NCB	Call on Credit
2Y	3,100.0	1,565.0	1,535.0	15,350.0
WS	4,000.0	1,570.0	2,430.0	24,300.0
MN	1,757.5	757.5	1,000.0	10,000.0
CH	552.5	52.5	500.0	5,000.0
LS	552.5	52.5	500.0	5,000.0
3S	150.0	–	150.0	1,500.0
2D	866.6	–	866.6	8,666.0
3B	500.0	–	500.0	5,000.0
WT	104.2	–	104.2	1,042.0
PT	26.3	–	26.3	263.0
ES	100.0	–	100.0	1,000.0
US	500.0	–	500.0	5,000.0
UT	200.0	–	200.0	2,000.0
SV	50.0	–	50.0	500.0
Total	12,459.6	3,997.5	8,462.1	84,621.0

ed a need for a call on credit of $25 million, and had then added a 100 per cent safety factor to get to $50 million. Although the company's financial management knew that there was no assurance that the mechanically calculated $84.6 million would in fact be available in an emergency situation, the company saw no need for a secondary safety factor of the magnitude of the one indicated — $34.6 million more than the objective of $50 million. Because of the potential for rearranging its Southwestern region banking, financial management did not want to count on the $8.666 million indicated for the Second National Bank of Dallas. Nor did the company want to utilize the Philadelphia Trust in a credit role unless absolutely required. By eliminating these two from the call list, Ancama calculated that it had a call on $75.7 million, which still provided more safety than was felt necessary.

After a good deal of consideration, Ancama decided that, if other constraints relating to the activity costs allowed, it would reduce balances at the banks listed in Table 3.13. These reductions would decrease Ancama's call on credit by $14.5 million, from $75.7 million to $61.2 million. Although

**Table 3.13. Proposed Reductions in Average NCB
(thousands of dollars)**

	Uncommitted NCB Before Reductions	Reductions
3B	500.0	350.0
LS	500.0	350.0
MN	1,000.0	750.0
Total	2,000.0	1,450.0

still well over its predicted need, Ancama's management was willing to see the firm maintain this high reserve pending a forthcoming study of the firm's over-all lock-box activity.

If the planned reductions had reflected balances that were surplus to each bank, the savings would be obvious. At Ancama's cost of capital, the savings would total (0.016667)($1,450,000) or $24,167.15 per month. But, except for Merchants National, the individual banks selected did not appear to have excess NCB; it was obvious that in the short run the necessity of providing compensation to 3B and LS to cover activity costs would prevent achievement of the full savings.

Let us look at the reallocation of variables made by CASH ALPHA after the new, reduced constraints are introduced, when we move from the prior case, designated Alternate 1 in Appendix D to a new case in which the reduced constraints are used, designated Alternate 2 in Appendix D.[3]

---

[3] Note that the comparison is with the next preceding case, *not* with the base case.

At MN the only change is a reduction of BAL of $750,000, which is the maximum relaxation allowed by the new constraint.

The situation is more complex at 3B. We have reduced the constraint on 3BNCB from $\geq$ $500,000 to $\geq$ $150,000. Thus we expect unallocated tax payments to displace at least a portion of the $350,000 potential reduction in balances. But we soon run into another constraint. Ancama's agreement with 3B calls for the value of tax payments to be equal to or less than one-third of total value of compensation to the bank. Total cost at 3B is $1,199.20. Thus the value of tax payments cannot exceed (1/3)($1,199.20) or $399.73, assuming that we do not want to pay more compensation for services rendered at this bank than is necessary. At the VTP level 3B of 0.000917, this means that taxes are constrained out when they reach the $399.73/0.000917, or the $435,913.78 level. Thus the increase in taxes from Alternate 1 to Alternate 2 is only $37,113.35. The value of this added amount at 3B is $34.03, which allows a reduction of balances there that would have earned $34.03. As the VNB factor at 3B is 0.001667, balances can be reduced by $34.03/0.001667, or $20,415.67.

This is hardly a satisfactory solution for Ancama. Instead of a $350,000 reduction in balances, all that can be reduced is $20,415.67. Ancama might at this point attempt a renegotiation at 3B, which would allow compensation through cash fees, and perhaps a relaxation of the constraint on use of tax payments. However, we shall leave 3B as it is for the present. When we make a systematic study of the totality of Ancama's retail lock-box activity in Alternate 4, we shall show how the reductions hoped for at 3B can take place by a reallocation of lock-box business away from this bank.

The effects at LS are still more complicated. As there were no book balances at LS before Alternate 2 was run, there could be no reduction in this factor. The float created by the Chicago Accounting Center payroll account of (0.15185)($4,320,000) or $655,992.00, less CTN at LS of $347,518.47, provided irreducible NCB at LS of $308,473.53. Service-charge credit on these balances totaled (0.00174)($308,473.53) or $536.74, more than enough to offset LSCST of $495.00. Thus all general disbursements that had been made through LS could be shunted elsewhere. The only disbursement activity left at LS was the $4,320,000 of payroll disbursements.

As was the case at 3B, the result at LS fell short of the desired $350,000 reduction in NCB. Instead, NCB dropped from $552,500.00 to $308,473.53, a reduction of $244,026.47. At this point, Ancama might have directed more WLB activity from CH to LS, so as to soak up the excess earnings on payroll float, or it might have opened a second payroll account at another bank for the Chicago Accounting Center, so that the excess NCB at LS could be diverted to release BAL or TAX or FEE elsewhere in the system. CASH ALPHA case studies would show which was preferable. For simplicity's sake, we shall leave LS at this admittedly suboptimal level throughout the balance of this study.

The final shifts in this Alternate 2 case affect CH. All of the $1,197,558.37 released by CASH ALPHA from LS is reallocated to CH. As the CH factor for conversion of disbursements to balances is 0.19459, the increased disbursements result in increased balances of (0.19459)($1,197,558.37), or $233,032.88, which allows a reduction of book balances at CH of the same amount. But by increasing disbursement activity at CH, costs there go up, from $3,187.58 in Alternate 1 to $3,218.54 in Alternate 2, an increase of $30.96. As our formula for CXP at CH is 0.000517 CHDIS, we expect a shift of $1,197,558.37 to result in additional checks on CH equal to (0.00517) ($1,197,558.37), or 619.13 checks which, at 5¢ per check, result in an additional cost of $30.96. (Fractional checks are obviously unrealistic, but they cause only a trivial distortion of resource allocation.) As we should expect from our inspection of CH in the base case, one-third of the added cost is made up by additional tax payments ($5,083.22, worth $10.32) and two-thirds by additional cash fees ($20.64).

Without taking other steps, this case of reduced call on credit is only a partial success. Measured at the 20 per cent opportunity cost, monthly savings over Alternate 1 are $16,703.42, not the $24,167.15 that would have resulted had Ancama been able to reduce book balances by the full $1,450,000. Book balances went down by $1,003,448.56, for a savings of $16,724.27 at the 20 per cent opportunity cost. This was offset in part by increased cash fees of $20.64.

Ancama ended the exercise with more borrowing potential at 3B and LS than it felt it wanted but maintained it because of the necessity of keeping balances at these banks in order to comply with constraints limiting the use of tax payments and cash fees at them. In a real-life situation, this might be considered a transient phase requiring correction. In this example, partial correction takes place when we test Alternate 4, a heuristic test of a new lock-box in Atlanta.

3.7. The Potential Savings of Renegotiation at 2D

Ancama's next use of CASH ALPHA was to measure the potential savings that could be obtained if it could successfully renegotiate terms at 2D to the charge/credit level used by CH. Management concern focused on 2D because of the high marginal cost of 29.9¢ for processing RLB there, which indicated the uneconomic nature of this relationship on the existing terms for Ancama. This concern was reinforced by the high fee-equivalent charge at 2D, which indicated that 2D costs were out-of-line even if viewed from an absolute rather than a systems standpoint.

The savings inherent in renegotiating 2D charge/credit terms to the CH level are, however, not obvious. It is not enough to take the CH terms and use them to revalue costs and compensation at 2D, on the basis that there will be no change in the *composition* of compensation throughout the system. If we did this we should find savings but not the full savings possible by using 2D as a more flexible component of our banking system.

Let us look one by one at the changes that take place as we move from our prior case to a new case in which 2D uses the same credit/charge schedule as does CH, designated Alternate 3 in Appendix D.

The first thing to note is the reduction in cost as measured by the bank's monthly analysis statement. 2DCST moves down from $2,107.88 in Alternate 2 to $1,714.07 in Alternate 3. The bulk of this change is due to lower RLB costs. Having made a first calculation of new CST at 2D, CASH ALPHA investigates the possibility of reallocating forms of compensation throughout the system.

As there were unallocated tax payments (HQTAX) in Alternate 2, which are "free" in the objective function, CASH ALPHA understandably reaches for some of these to pay for services at 2D, because 2D is now, in our wishful analysis, willing to take tax payments for service-charge credit on the CH basis. The Alternate 3 solution shows $281,456.74 of tax payments going to 2D. As tax payments carry a value of 0.00203 2DTAX, the $281,456.74 is worth $571.36, which is exactly one-third of 2DCST. This is what we should expect: tax payments are constrained out at the one-third of TVL level at 2D, as at CH. TVL equals CST because there are no constraints at 2D that would cause TVL to exceed CST. We also note that the new CASH ALPHA solution calls for 2DFEE to be $571.36 — also one-third of 2DCST and as high as it can go on the CH basis without violating the constraint on cash fees.

The balance of CST at 2D, or $571.36, must be paid for by service-charge credit on balances. Because Dallas creates more float per dollar of disbursements than any other Chicago Accounting Center bank, it is not surprising that CASH ALPHA calls for all the balances at 2D to take the form of float. The solution calls for a zero book balance and DIS of $1,173,047.71. Balances created by DIS of this amount are equal to (0.22593)($1,173,047.71), or $265,026.67. After subtracting 2DCTN of $104,802.64, 2DNCB equals $160,224.03. At the CH value for NCB of 0.003566 NCB, NCB at 2D have a value of $571.36, which we could have expected as it is also one-third of TVL.

But these rearrangements in our dealings with 2D cause other system dislocations. First, disbursements at 2D have dropped from $4,299,647.79 in Alternate 2 to the level of $1,173,047.71. Where will the $3,126,600.08

of disbursements that had been made through 2D now be made? The first thing we note is that $2,984,318.34 of disbursements have been shunted to CH, thus reducing BAL at CH to the zero point. But when we do this, we increase CST at CH by drawing more checks on this bank. The effects are similar to those outlined in the discussion of Alternate 2. Additional costs of $77.14 are offset one-third by additional tax payments of $12,667.42, worth $25.71, and two-thirds by additional cash fees of $51.43.

There are still $142,281.74 of Chicago Accounting Center disbursements left over. CASH ALPHA allocates these to 2Y, creating balances at 2Y of (0.20594)($142,281.74) or $29,301.50. But because BAL at 2Y were zero before these additional Chicago Accounting Center disbursements were brought into solution, the additional $29,301.50 of balances cannot be used to reduce book balances there. Thus, there is an opportunity to make an advantageous rearrangement of headquarters disbursements. CASH ALPHA moves $137,759.77 of headquarters disbursements out of 2Y (making room for the $142,281.74 of Chicago Accounting Center disbursements) and into MN. This latter step allows book balances at MN to be cut by $27,315.01 without disturbing the net collected balance level there, and it leaves NCB at 2Y at the level of $3,100,000.

Table 3.14 shows the effects of the changes in Alternate 3. As shown in

Table 3.14. Net Results of Alternate 3 Shifts

Book balances	-$608,033.52
Unallocated tax payments	-$294,124.16
Cash fees	+$ 622.79

Appendix D, the savings have a value of $9,508.36 per month on a 20 per cent pretax opportunity cost basis, or $2,414.43 on a 6 per cent pretax opportunity cost basis. In either case incentive for renegotiation is clearly present.

In the course of renegotiation with 2D, several CASH ALPHA case studies might be run to show relative values of various combinations of renegotiated terms. For example, a proposed revision of terms by 2D might form the basis of a new CASH ALPHA run. Based on that new run, the company could perhaps see from the present shadow prices where slight changes in the proposed terms could result in significant cost changes to the company. In the 2D case, for example, in view of the significance of tax payments, the company might push strongly to have the bank accept tax payments for service-charge credit but be somewhat less insistent on achieving the CH per item price levels.

This example illustrates the systems nature of CASH ALPHA. Although all the renegotiation in Alternate 3 takes place at 2D, the significant savings appear to show up at CH and MN, where the large cuts in book balances take place. The savings are *systems* savings, *made* at 2D which *show up* at CH and MN.

4 REDESIGNING THE BANKING SYSTEM

4.1. The Role of Structural Change

We take as our starting point in this case a successful renegotiation with 2D, with 2D adopting in all respects the credit/charge schedule tested in Alternate 3. In a hypothetical case such as this, it is easy to move instantly from one major renegotiation to the next, thus creating, perhaps, an impression of an even less permanence of the credit/charge terms that exist between bank and customer than in fact truly exist. Three points should perhaps be made. The first is that each case that I describe is an attempt to illustrate a use of the CASH ALPHA algorithm. The use of a single company in all examples makes possible what I feel is an interesting explanation of some CASH ALPHA uses, and it enables me to show how a system could evolve. But my intent is to focus more on the mechanism itself than on normative rules for banking relations, although I am aware of the extent to which this study includes my own value judgments on how bank-customer relations should be structured. I would not want to give the impression of a normative stand in favor or repeated abrupt shifts in a firm's banking relations. Certainly no treasurer would relish the job of arranging major shifts in the way his firm does business with his banks shortly after a major change has taken place. This leads to my second point. CASH ALPHA provides for the most efficient allocation of resources given the ground rules that exist at any particular time. Thus it seems to me that it is very well suited to an *evolutionary development* of more efficient cash systems.

It is not necessary to change one's business radically to get value out of CASH ALPHA. There is apparently great potential value in using CASH ALPHA simply as a short-term planning tool to allocate variables. But it also seems to be a very powerful tool in assessing structural change, and this leads me to my third point. *I believe that structural change is a major managerial responsibility.* If a firm's management can see significant savings from the adoption of structural change in any of its systems or subsystems, it *should* adopt those changes. Good tactics may call for a gradual transition, but the changes should neverthe- less be made. A bank's strength in resisting structural change is a function of its competitive position and the chance circumstances that shape the bank customers' business systems. This last point should become clear in the last of the CASH ALPHA cases.

4.2. Heuristic Testing of a New Lock-Box

Georgia First National Bank, an aggressive Atlanta bank, approached Ancama some months after 2D had agreed to the CH charge/credit structure. Georgia First National was eager to have Ancama's Southeastern retail lock-box business, and offered to process RLB on the following basis:

1. Ancama would maintain average NCB of at least $100,000.
2. NCB would earn service-charge credit at the rate of .0025 per month (3 per cent per year).
3. RLB would be handled for 4.25¢ each, CXP for 5¢, and CXD for 2¢.
4. The bank would charge a $75 monthly "overhead" fee, which would cover postage, wire transfers, and miscellaneous items.
5. Ancama would have the option of using earnings credit on NCB or cash fees, or a combination of both, to compensate GF for its services. (Of course, a portion of the compensation to the bank would always take the form of balances, because of the requirement for average NCB of at least $100,000).

In order to evaluate the attractiveness of this offer, Ancama made a thorough study of the pattern of mailings of its retail lock-box items, and then applied a heuristic test inspired by Levy's approach.[1]

Appendixes E.1 through E.5 show a summary of Ancama's survey. The figures used in this "survey" are not based on an actual analysis of mail times or in- transit times. They are simply numbers that are useful in illustrating the problem and the proposed solution.

The sample made by Ancama categorizes all incoming retail lock-box items by twenty-four geographic regions. Average mail times from each region to

---

[1] Ferdinand K. Levy, "An Application of Heuristic Problem Solving to Accounts Receivable Management," *Management Science,* Vol. 12, No. 6 (February, 1966), pp. B-236-B-244.

each lock-box bank have been calculated, as have average in-transit times from each lock-box bank back to an average of banks in the area. For example, Appendix E.3 shows that there were 918 items from Ohio in the sample. The average Ohio remittance in the sample was $41.98. The indicated volume from Ohio during a normal month, based on sample data, is 10,439 items. Mail time on average from customers to CH (the lock-box bank for Ohio) is estimated at 1.60 days. Post office data could be used to develop figures such as the artificial 1.60 figure used here. Alternately, independent mail sampling data could be helpful. Post office data normally show pertinent train and plane schedule times. However, it does not provide a basis for estimating system delays, if any, and it does not normally provide as fine a screen as a company might want. The ZIP-code system provides the basis for a most comprehensive test program of mail times. The major commercial banks have probably done more work in this area than anyone else.

Mail times are calculated from each area to *each* lock-box bank, not just to the lock-box bank that normally services the area. In-transit times are also estimated for each RLB bank in the system to each of the twenty-four geographic districts. For Ohio, in-transit time from CH is estimated at 1.85 days. One bank, 3B, gives automatic one-day availability on all lock-box items. In-transit time estimates are based on Federal Reserve schedules of availability, as amended by bank willingness to quote faster availability schedules based on their own ability to expedite the collection of deposits.

With these data in hand, and a few amended equations, CASH ALPHA can develop the best possible distribution of lock-box items as well as the best possible allocation of tax payments, disbursements, and fees. But before amending the equations, let us digress for a moment on the value of expediting the collection of receivables.

A firm's investment in receivables tends to be a fixed asset, from an economic point of view, despite the accounting classification of receivables as a current asset. Obviously, short-term creditors look to the liquidation of receivables as a prime source of cash for debt repayment, and thus it is proper to account them as a current asset. But as receivables are constantly replaced with new receivables, the stable or growing firm has, in economic terms, a permanent investment in receivables. Leaving aside the question of the cost of seasonal bulges in a firm's receivables, any change in the level of receivables is either a source or use of capital at the firm's opportunity cost. Sales growth normally carries with it the necessity for a firm to invest more capital in receivables. More important for our purpose here, any program which reduces the firm's investment in receivables makes available cash that can be reinvested in the business at the firm's opportunity rate.

The timing of payment of a receivable is beyond a creditor's control until the customer mails his check. There are influences that can be brought to bear to make customers pay their bills promptly, but it is basically true that there is little the firm can do to reduce accounts receivable (without reducing sales) *until* the customer places his check in the mail.[2] But then, all other things being equal, the firm will want to shorten the total time from the moment the check is dropped in the mail until it has been collected. The firm utilizing a lock-box system is thus interested in two times – mail time from the mail box to a lock-box bank, and in-transit time from the lock-box bank back to the paying bank.

In his method, Levy calculates the variable cost of each check collected, based on mail time, in-transit time, the variable charge per item handled by the bank, and the interest rate to the firm, for each of many money center banks (Levy lists eighteen cities) that the firm might use. In his example he sums the cost of variables as if all checks went through each bank. To the sum so calculated for each bank he adds the fixed monthly cost of doing business with that bank. From the several summations, Levy can select the *one* bank that would provide the cheapest lock-box service to the firm, if the firm chose to do business with only one lock-box bank. Levy then assigns all checks whose collection costs are absolutely minimum to the selected lock-box. He repeats the process, making a new summation of all variable costs for all checks *not* assigned to the first bank, adding the fixed monthly costs of doing business with each, and determining which is the logical second bank for the firm. All checks whose collection costs are minimum at the second bank are assigned there, and all remaining checks are tentatively assigned to the two banks on the basis of the lesser cost between the two. The total cost of this allocation – fixed costs at the two banks as well as variable costs – are compared with the total cost of a one-bank solution. If the cost is greater with two lock-boxes than with one, then only the first bank is used. If the cost is less with two lock-boxes, then Levy will continue to "deal off the top" until the addition of one more bank results in an increase in costs.

It seems to me that there is a major problem in Levy's approach of treating the banks simply as adjuncts to a receivables system. For many firms there will be other considerations that will make them most reluctant to wipe the slate clean of established banking relationships. The banking system, as a system, has values to the firm apart from the collection of receivables, which, I postulate, are chiefly related to the firm's need for access to credit on short notice. Thus it appears to me that the selection of lock-box banks, and the territories they serve, can be better determined by making the routing of lock-box items an independent variable in the CASH ALPHA algorithm, which will minimize the cost of the company's lock-box system *consistent with all other constraints relating to the banking system* that company management may

---

[2] This, however, is changing. For example, several insurance companies are at present using drafts directed to their customers' banks to collect insurance premiums.

feel appropriate. To make the routing of lock-box items an independent variable, it is necessary to change some of the CASH ALPHA equations. The needed changes are now explained.

All earlier cases have carried a fixed factor, TORCV, of \$494,054.00. This was an estimate for a normal month of the average investment that Ancama had in receivables during the period from the time the customers' checks were dropped in the mail until they were processed by the RLB banks. I assume here that processing an item at a bank and the capability of posting the receipt of funds on the company's ledger occur on the same day, although this is not universally practical today. The TORCV was a constant in all earlier CASH ALPHA runs, because the pattern of deposits was always the same: all Ohio items went to Chicago, all Texas items to Dallas, and so on.

We shall now reroute lock-box items to gain the lowest total system costs, which may result in either an increase or a decrease in TORCV — it is not intuitively obvious which it will be before the computer run is made. So we need to describe TORCV in a new way:

$$TORCV = 2DRCV + 3BRCV + CHRCV + GFRCV + PTRCV + USRCV$$

The individual bank RCV's can be formulated once we have formulated the distribution of lock-box items. Heretofore we have used "RLB" to express the number of retail lock-box items processed by a bank in a given month. Thus one earlier equation, a prediction equation, stated that $3BRLB = 0.0336$, which meant that we expected 33,600 items to flow through the Third National Bank of Boston. From Appendix E.2, we see that 3B was the lock-box for all retail billings in New England — except southern Connecticut — and upstate New York, or Areas A and F. If we describe all retail lock-box items that flow from Area A to 3B as "3BARL" and similarly all items that flow from Area F to 3B as "3BFRL," then, in the normal month, $3BRLB = 3BARL + 3BFRL = 0.0336$. More generally, all items that *might* flow from all geographic areas through 3B would be described by the following equation:

$$3BRLB = 3BARL + 3BBRL + \ldots + 3BXRL$$

For each combination of geographic area and lock-box, we can calculate an investment coefficient from the test data, which will approximate the average monthly investment in receivables from that area processed through that lock-box. For example, let us consider 3B and Area A again. The investment coefficient would be calculated as follows:

$$\text{Average value of retail lock-box items} \quad \times \quad \frac{\text{Mail days from Area A to 3B}}{\text{Average days in month}}$$

or $(\$42.16)(1.38/30.4167) = \$1.91$

What this means is that for each retail lock-box item flowing from Area A through 3B during a normal month, there is an average investment in accounts receivable of $1.91 — from mailing by the customer to capability of posting the receipt of payment on the accounts receivable ledger. Similarly, Appendix E.2 shows that an item from Area F to 3B would carry an investment coefficient of $2.67, and the unlikely combination of Area X (southern California, Arizona, and New Mexico) and 3B would carry an investment coefficient of $6.70. The general equation for 3BRCV is thus described by a listing of all areas, with the coefficients that have been calculated for each combination, as follows:

$$3BRCV = 1.91\ 3BARL + 1.92\ 3BBRL + \ldots + 6.7\ 3BXRL$$

It is also necessary to aggregate the items sent from each area to all lock-boxes. For example, Appendix E.2 shows that in a normal month 26,006 items flow from Area A. Thus a description of all possible flows from an area in a normal month would be

$$2DARL + 3BARL + CHARL + GFARL + PTARL + USARL = .026006$$

It is also necessary to redefine our equations for in-transit items. In earlier runs, we simply applied a coefficient to deposits. For example, we described $3BCTN = 0.032877\ 3BDEP$. In a normal month, deposits at 3B totaled $1,895,000, so CTN equaled (0.032877) ($1,895,000), or $62,301.91. When we break down retail lock-box receipts as we have just done, we shall still have some other deposits that are normally deposited over the counter into 3B by the Boston Accounting Center.

How do we calculate CTN on RLB items? For each combination of geographic area and lock-box, we can calculate an *in-transit coefficient* from test data and our knowledge of in-transit times, which will approximate the average monthly investment in in-transit items from that bank for that area. The calculation is exactly the same as for the investment coefficient, except that in-transit time in days from the bank to the area is substituted for mail days from the area to the bank. Returning to our example of 3B and Area A, the in-transit coefficient would be

$$\frac{\text{Average value of retail lock-box items processed}}{} \times \frac{\text{Days in transit from 3B to Area A}}{\text{Average days in month}}$$

or $(\$42.16)\ (1.00/30.4167) = \$1.39$

Note again the one-day availability factor given by 3B. The in-transit coefficient refers to the basis on which each bank calculates availability, not on the actual time that collection may take.

In reforming CTN equations, we can write an equation for each bank that gives effect to the different in-transit coefficients for each combination and that will also give effect to the other deposits made in each of the retail lock-box banks. For example, our formulation of CTN for 3B is now as follows:

$$3BCTN = 1.39\ 3BARL + 2.5\ 3BBRL + \ldots + 2.97\ 3BXRL + 0.032887\ 3BOTC$$

3BOTC refers to the *dollars* deposited by Ancama in 3B other than through lock-box deposits.

We now have the basic data necessary to rerun CASH ALPHA, based on a typical month, with knowledge of the pattern of retail lock-box sendings, to see whether addition of GF would lower total system costs.

4.3. The Test Results

Our first interest is in seeing how CASH ALPHA has reallocated RLB items. Tables 4.1 and 4.2 show the results:

Table 4.1. Reallocation of RLB Items — Test of GF Lock-Box

Area	Number of Items Monthly	Lock-Box Bank Before Test	After Test
A New England (except southern Connecticut)	26,006	3B	3B (6,129) PT (19,877)
B Metropolitan New York City	8,035	PT	PT
C Mid-Atlantic	6,926	PT	PT
D Ohio	10,439	CH	CH
E Western Pennsylvania and West Virginia	2,749	PT	PT
F Upstate New York	7,594	3B	PT
G Metropolitan Chicago and northern Illinois	21,849	CH	CH
H Southern Illinois, Indiana, and Iowa	4,687	CH	CH
I Michigan	11,563	CH	CH
J Wisconsin	7,037	CH	CH
K Virginia	1,735	PT	PT
L Tennessee and Kentucky	5,665	CH	GF (1,512) PT (4,153)
M North Carolina	2,066	PT	PT
N South Carolina and Georgia	2,289	PT	GF
O Alabama and Mississippi	7,314	2D	CH
P Florida	9,291	2D	PT
Q Texas	10,901	2D	CH
R Arkansas and Oklahoma	8,479	2D	CH
S Louisiana	6,515	2D	CH
T Missouri, Kansas, Eastern Colorado, Nebraska, and Wyoming	6,388	CH	CH
U Minnesota, North Dakota, South Dakota, Montana, and Idaho	5,372	CH	CH
V Washington and Oregon	7,874	US	US
W Northern California, Nevada, Utah, and western Colorado	17,213	US	US
X Southern California, New Mexico, and Arizona	30,013	US	US

Table 4.2. Bank-by-Bank Changes in Alternate 4

Code and Area	Before Test Items per Month	After Test Items per Month	Comment
CH			
D Ohio	10,439	10,439	–
G Metropolitan Chicago	21,849	21,849	–
H Southern Illinois, Indiana and Iowa	4,687	4,687	–
I Michigan	11,563	11,563	–
J Wisconsin	7,037	7,037	–
L Tennessee and Kentucky	5,665	–	lost to GF and PT
T Missouri, Kansas, eastern Colorado, Nebraska, Wyoming	6,388	6,388	–
U Minnesota, ND, SD, Montana, Idaho	5,372	5,372	–
O Alabama and Mississippi	–	7,314	gained from 2D
Q Texas	–	10,901	gained from 2D
R Arkansas and Oklahoma	–	8,479	gained from 2D
S Louisiana	–	6,515	gained from 2D
Total	73,000	100,544	
3B			
A New England (except southern Connecticut)	26,006	6,129	19,877 lost to PT
F Upstate New York	7,594	–	lost to PT
Total	33,600	6,129	
PT			
B Metropolitan New York City	8,035	8,035	–
C Mid-Atlantic	6,926	6,926	–
E Western Pennsylvania and West Virginia	2,749	2,749	–
K Virginia	1,735	1,735	–
M North Carolina	2,066	2,066	–
N South Carolina and Georgia	2,289	–	lost to GF
A New England (except southern Connecticut)	–	19,877	gained from 3B
F Upstate New York	–	7,594	gained from 3B
L Tennessee and Kentucky	–	4,153	gained from CH
P Florida	–	9,291	gained from 2D
Total	23,800	62,426	
2D			
O Alabama and Mississippi	7,314	–	lost to CH
P Florida	9,291	–	lost to PT
Q Texas	10,901	–	lost to CH
R Arkansas and Iklahoma	8,479	–	lost to PT
S Louisiana	6,515	–	lost to CH
Total	42,500	–	
US			
V Washington and Oregon	7,874	7,874	–
W Northern California, Nevada, Utah, Western Colorado	17,213	17,213	–
X Southern California, New Mexico, Arizona	30,013	30,013	–
Total	55,100	55,100	
GF			
L Tennessee and Kentucky	–	1,512	gained from CH
N South Carolina and Georgia	–	2,289	gained from PT
Total	–	3,801	

Let us examine the changes that have taken place as shown in these tables and in Appendix D. At the outset it is important to note that some of the changes in this computer run reflect the introduction of the GF variables, but some do not — they reflect the freedom that the algorithm now has in selecting the best bank for RLB items, given the constraints within which the banking system works.

Let us first look at the introduction of GF. When we introduce the new constraint, GFNCB $\geq$ $100,000.00, we insure that *some* activity will flow through GF to use up the service-charge credit generated by the $100,000.00. We note from the computer printout for this case (the printout for this case is not reproduced in the appendixes) that GFTVL and GFCST are both $250.00, which is exactly 0.25 per cent of $100,000.00, the bank's monthly allowance for NCB. CASH ALPHA has subtracted the $75.00 monthly overhead from the $250.00, and then sought to use the service-charge credit balance of $175.00 to pay for the cost of processing RLB items and checks paid. The solution shows 269 checks paid at 5¢ per check and 3,801 RLB items at 4.25¢ for a total cost of $175.00. The selection of RLB items is not wholly obvious. We should expect that Area N (South Carolina and Georgia) items would flow through GF, but we should not necessarily expect a portion of Area L (Tennessee and Kentucky) instead of a portion of Area P (Florida) checks to make up the difference. The delta-j's for this case show that adding one RLB item from Area L to CH (and thus taking it from GF) involves a system cost of about ¼¢ (CHLRL = 0.00253664). And taking one RLB item from Area P away from PT and assigning it to GF would cost the system about ½¢ (GFPRL = 0.00508582).

Our tentative conclusion at this point is that the GF offer is not particularly attractive to Ancama, despite the considerable systems savings indicated in Appendix D. (Total monthly cost goes from $92,115.46 in Alternate 4 to $88,501.33 in Alternate 5, a saving of $3,614.13). Since GF attracted no more activity than that necessary to soak up the service-charge credit on the minimum $100,000.00, it appears that the system would have made a different allocation had it been free to select the NCB level there.

What happens to 2D in this example is interesting. When 2D does an active RLB business, OMC (other monthly costs) are predicted at $90.00 per month. In Alternate 4 there are no RLB items left at 2D. But the CASH ALPHA program still carries the $90.00 as a fixed cost, so CASH ALPHA calculated sufficient revenues (in the form of service-charge credit on balances and tax payments) to defray these costs. The run shows us that, based on the introduction of the GF variables, it is no longer economic to use 2D. To have a clean solution, the case should be rerun with 2DOMC of $90.00 deleted. The changes in the solution against Alternate 4 as calculated will be minor.

Have we proved that we should close out the relationship with 2D and open an account with GF? Absolutely not! But neither have we proved that the old solution was necessarily any better. The changes that took place between Alternate 3 and Alternate 4 obviously seem to be related to the rearrangement of RLB items. Consider what happened to 3B in Alternative 4. In Alternate 3 we had attempted to reduce NCB at 3B by $350,000, in line with the re-evaluation of the company's need for credit. But NCB dropped only $20,415.67, not $350,000. This was because we had arbitrarily assigned all New England (except southern Connecticut) and all upstate New York RLB to 3B. This created a fixed requirement for generation of service-charge credit at 3B which blocked the reduction of balances. In Alternate 4, CASH ALPHA is free to reallocate RLB variables to minimize system costs, and it reallocates all upstate New York and most New England items away from 3B to PT. 3BNCB falls to $150,000 the new constraint level, and it is only because this constraint exists that more RLB do not leave for PT. How logical is it to move RLB originating in New England out of a Boston lock-box and into a Philadelphia lock-box? The marginal value of 3BRLB (from the computer printout of the case, which is not reproduced in the appendixes) is 5.44¢ and the marginal value of PTRLB is 0.02¢. If our credit needs can be achieved with a minimum of $150,000 at 3B, then the lower costs at PT, and PT's willingness to take additional tax payments (there are still HQTAX left to be allocated), far outweigh the mail time and in-transit time advantage provided by 3B.

The rest of the changes in Alternate 4 seem obvious. US retains all of the West Coast RLB business it had before Alternate 5. The other system changes reflect a reshuffling of means of compensation to achieve an optimal solution, similar to the reshuffling described in detail when we considered Alternates 2 and 3.

Where does this leave us? We have shown that changes from Alternate 3 are in order, but we are not sure what changes we should make. At this point, management must decide which tests may be appropriate to reach a solution. One obvious test would be to remove the GF equations altogether and see how CASH ALPHA would allocate RLB items among CH, PT, US, 3B, and 2D. It seems quite possible that 2D would be allocated out by CASH ALPHA even without having GF in, but this is not obvious. Such a case and Alternate 4 (refined by the removal of 2DOMC of $90.00) would form the basis for a decision, *if* the minimum average NCB requirement at GF were, in fact, a fixed requirement. It might be possible to negotiate for a smaller minimum average NCB there. Right-hand-side ranging of this solution (not reproduced in the appendixes) shows us that if we vary the fixed NCB at GF below $72,750 we shall run out of lock-box items from Area L (Tennessee and Kentucky) and thus need a new system calculation of variables. It would be valuable, I think, to run a case in which Alternate 4 is repeated with omission of the $100,000 minimum average balance at GF. This run would show the terms on which a relationship with GF would be attractive to Ancama, and thus would provide the basis for negotiations with GF (if, in fact, there is a level at which GF is attractive to Ancama).

The computer cannot decide, using CASH ALPHA, which tests to run. Management must still ask, "Well, what if . . .?" and then CASH ALPHA can be used to furnish a fast, cheap answer. (See Chapter 5, Section 5.7, for a discussion of the cost of CASH ALPHA runs.) CASH ALPHA focuses financial management's time on the determination of constraints — what is important to the firm in structuring its relations with the banking community — and on the selection of possible structural changes that might be tested.

An interesting technical problem is raised by Alternate 4 in the splitting of a regional area between two lock-box banks. Areas A and L are both split, Area A items going to 3B and PT and Area L items to GF and PT. For simplicity's sake, a firm could simply ignore the minority bank and send out all bills with a return envelope to the majority bank. In the short run, this would seem to be cheaper than to adapt the system each month for shifts to an optimal solution. But it may be possible to adapt the billing process so that a predetermined number of billings going to one regional area would get a green envelope (Bank A) and another group a blue envelope (Bank B). Alternatively, a window envelope might be used with the proper lock-box address printed on the return card by the computer. A somewhat more sophisticated system would shunt the lower value billings to those banks in which there was a large predetermined balance level that could be used to offset service charges, while the higher value billings went to the banks where mail times and in-transit times would be lower. This in turn would create a ledger posting problem. Consider the case of PT, a Boston Accounting Center bank. Each day (using Alternate 4) Boston would receive payment data from PT on a few retail customers from Tennessee and Kentucky whose accounts were lodged with the Chicago Accounting Center. Rather than have PT communicate these data directly to the Chicago Accounting Center, it would seem logical for the Boston Accounting Center to relay payment information once each day to the Chicago Accounting Center. In a complex, multibank system, a daily "clearing house" operation through the headquarters computer center might be appropriate. I am assuming here that each of the lock-box banks has the ability to transmit by wire a daily magnetic tape of payment data to the accounting centers.

Alternate 4 is not an ideal case. I think that the refinement suggested in Section 4.4 has greater potential value, although after a point this latter method is no more than a series of case studies to determine a course of action. What Alternate 4 *does* show is the practicality of integrating accounts receivable decisions with banking policy decisions rather than having each made on different economic bases.

4.4. An Alternate Heuristic Test

The approach described in the previous two sections can be a powerful tool in analyzing the economic effect of adding an additional lock-box bank. But the siting of an additional bank may not always be as obvious as it seemed in the Ancama example. This section discusses a methof for developing insights as to which banking center cities might best be used by a company in the light of its own peculiar collection pattern *and* its own long-established policies with respect to its major banks.

Let us assume that a firm, Company Y, identifies thirty cities as potentially attractive collection points. At present Company Y has lock-boxes with three banks in three of these cities. Two of these banks are important to the firm for credit support and for other intangible services rendered; the third acts, essentially, as a data-processing center for the company. Consequently, the firm is insistent upon maintaining important relationships with the two banks but not necessarily with the third.

If the Levy approach can be described as "dealing off the top," then the use of CASH ALPHA in this example could best be described as "dealing out a full deck." Company Y wants to see the best distribution of all lock-box items if it uses all thirty banks. By inspection of the results it so obtains it can eliminate those banks that appear to add little value to the system.

To make such a test, Company Y needs (1) a comprehensive study of the mail time and in-transit time of its incoming receivables, as was obtained in the Ancama example, and (2) credit/charge terms from banks in the selected test cities.

The mail time and in-transit time study is somewhat more complex than in the Ancama example, because of the larger number of cities from which and to which times must be calculated. The CASH ALPHA equations also grow much larger, necessitating the use of more computer time. The question of how much money to spend on this data collection and analysis portion of a banking structure study depends largely on the potential savings to be obtained. Some bankers have cautioned against anything but a 100 per cent sample in a study of a wholesale lock-box (individual items averaging $500 or $1,000 or more), but a much smaller sample should give satisfactory results for a retail lock-box system.

Establishing credit/charge terms for all the additional banks presents a different problem. It seems to me that Company Y should seek terms on the basis of a no-fixed-minimum balance, with the option of paying for services on a cash fee or deposit balance basis, and on a tax payment basis as well if possible. By having quotations on the basis of a no-fixed-minimum balance, one fixed cost of using each bank is eliminated, thus facilitating the first computer run by eliminating integer programming problems. There are other fixed costs, however, about which I shall say more shortly.

A possible first-run substitute for actual quotations would be the use of the credit/charge terms of a bank that does *not* have a major credit relationship with the company (which could lead to a distorted credit/charge schedule) but which has quoted cash fee terms with no balance requirements, as a surrogate for the credit/charge term for *all other* potential lock-box banks. Following a first analysis on this basis, discussions could be initiated with banks in those cities that CASH ALPHA indicates are attractive to test whether credit/charge terms approximating the assumed terms can actually be obtained. Failure to obtain the desired terms in one city would subsequently require a case-study approach using the best terms available in that city in comparison with combinations at banks in other cities that do quote attractive credit/charge terms.

Assuming that we have quotations from banks in each of the financial centers we want to test or that we have decided to use substitute credit/charge terms for banks in these cities, we then run the CASH ALPHA program. This run will show us where each area's mail should be directed assuming that there are no fixed costs to the company associated with the addition of additional banks. Although we know this assumption is false, it is useful to make a first run on this basis to develop insights for future tests.

The output of this first run *should* show some obviously impractical results. For example, the first run might, in part, show the following:[3]

Money Center City	Number of RLB Assigned Here in a Typical Month
Memphis	14,298
Nashville	2,207
Atlanta	17,557

What has happened here is that CASH ALPHA has assigned one small geographic area — perhaps one or two three-digit ZIP-code areas — or it has split off a portion of a larger area, and directed it to Nashville. By looking at the shadow price for RLB at the Nashville bank, we might find a marginal cost of 2.53¢ per item. Although we cannot be sure that the 2.53¢ will hold through 2,207 items, the number of items seems trivial enough so that there should be no problem in assuming such a cost. At this cost, the company would lose (2,207) ($0.0253), or $55.84, per month *before* consideration of fixed costs if it elected not to have a Nashville lock-box bank.

[3]The preceding figures and those that follow are simply numbers picked at random to demonstrate the points I want to make. I have *not* run a CASH ALPHA program for Company Y, as I did for Ancama.

But there are two categories of fixed costs to consider, one dealing with bank charges and the other dealing with the company's own costs. The National Bank of Chicago, in the Ancama case, provides a good example of bank fixed costs. In a normal month it charged Ancama $30 for wire transfers, a flat $25 for account reconciliation, and $35 for postage, for a total of $90. While postage would certainly vary with volume of business, the other two categories of expense very well might not. In the Ancama example, Georgia First quoted a flat $75 "overhead" fee to cover such items.

But there are further administrative costs within the company that tend to be fixed with the addition of new lock-box banks. It is far easier to track down mistakes when a company deals with one bank than when it deals with six banks. The fixed cost of adding one more bank is a function of the particular organization of each company, the work load of the people engaged in this part of the business, and the error experience that the type of business entails. The firm using CASH ALPHA in this test might either establish a fixed cost for each additional lock-box bank or assume no fixed costs, solve the problem, then determine whether the savings indicated by use of the additional bank more than offset a reasonable estimate of the fixed cost of adding the bank.

In the example of the Nashville bank, it is obviously uneconomic to add it to Company Y's system. The indicated savings do not even cover what could be expected in the way of normal bank fixed costs, let alone company fixed costs. But suppose the indicated savings before consideration of fixed costs came to $500 per month. If bank fixed costs are estimated at $75, as in the Georgia First example in the Ancama case, then the company would have to decide whether the savings of $425 after the bank fixed costs were sufficiently attractive to offset the incremental fixed costs of administering dealings with one more bank.

After inspection of the first run, Company Y might throw out the obviously uneconomic banks; it might then rerun the program to see what effect the rerouting of items that had previously been directed to obviously uneconomic banks might have on marginal banks. For example, in its first run Company Y received the following optimum allocation of RLB on a before-overhead basis:

Atlanta	17,557	Kansas	3,892	Omaha	-0-
Boston	-0-	Los Angeles†	31,613	Philadelphia	-0-
Buffalo	1,514	Louisville	-0-	Phoenix	2,987
Chicago*	70,122	Memphis	14,298	Pittsburgh	4,416
Cincinnati	-0-	Miami	10,010	Portland	3,615
Cleveland	3,914	Milwaukee	-0-	Richmond	4,975
Dallas	8,517	Minneapolis	196	St. Louis	-0-
Denver	3,090	Nashville	2,207	Salt Lake City	1,418
Detroit	-0-	New Orleans	8,412	San Francisco	17,014
Houston	5,020	New York*	89,012	Seattle	7,815
				Total	311,616

*Already lock-box cities, the relationship requires maintenance of a major account.

†Already a lock-box city, the relationship does *not* require a major account.

It is immediately apparent that the high balances that Company Y maintains in New York and Chicago have "swamped out" the possibility of doing lock-box business in Boston and Philadelphia, in the case of New York; and of doing business in Cincinnati, Detroit, Milwaukee, Omaha, and St. Louis, in the case of Chicago. This swamping out is a function of the policy level of balances at the two major banks as well as a function of charges quoted by all the banks. In areas of the country not dominated by a major credit-granting bank, the pattern of attractive lock-boxes is much more intricate. The best pattern seems to be two lock-boxes serving almost half of the firm's normal monthly volume — New York and Chicago — with several banks in other areas, each serving a much smaller area. Company Y could simply make an arbitrary cutoff at, say, 10,000 items per month and end up with seven lock-box banks. Alternatively, it might select an arbitrary "best" number of banks (say, six or eight), based on a rough assessment of the balance between the administrative costs of a complex system and the savings possible through the use of such a system, and then run multiple case studies in one computer session of *all* combinations of the "best" number of banks, perhaps excluding those banks that, from the first run, appear to be obviously uneconomic. If there are many apparently economic banks, however, the computer time needed for such a study could be prohibitive. To avoid this, Company Y simply reran the CASH ALPHA program after eliminating the obviously uneconomic banks, which it defined (based on calculations of incremental fixed costs per bank) as those collecting less than 2,500 items per month. The New CASH ALPHA run looked like this:

Atlanta	17,557	Los Angeles	31,613	Pittsburgh	5,930*
Chicago	70,320*	Memphis	16,505*	Portland	3,615
Cleveland	3,914	Miami	10,010	Richmond	4,975
Dallas	8,517	New Orleans	8,412	San Francisco	18,432*
Denver	3,090	New York	89,012	Seattle	7,815
Houston	5,020	Phoenix	2,987		
Kansas City	3,892			Total	311,616

*Changed from the last run.

Had Company Y set the minimum at 5,000 items per month for the second run, it would have eliminated both Cleveland and Pittsburgh, and it thus would have missed the possibility of allocating the Buffalo volume to Pittsburgh — which would make Pittsburgh an "economic" lock-box city.

Now Company Y should start on a series of case study tests designed to see whether the firm should narrow the number of lock-box banks still more. At this point I would insert the estimated fixed costs of doing business with each bank — both the bank's fixed charges and the firm's internal fixed costs. Then tests can be made of combinations that seem to make sense. For example, it looks as though the volume of items handled by Pittsburgh (5,930 per month) and Cleveland (3,914 per month) might well be combined. But it is not obvious whether the business is better concentrated in Pittsburgh or Cleveland, although the greater number of checks directed to Pittsburgh when they are both in solution would seem to favor it over Cleveland. CASH ALPHA will show which is better, however, by comparing a run that has Pittsburgh in and Cleveland out with one that has Cleveland in and Pittsburgh out. Similarly, the firm might want to test San Francisco, Portland, and Seattle. Also, as there are six Southern and Southwestern cities in the second CASH ALPHA run, Company Y might want to test possible combinations of two banks, or even possible combinations of three. While it seems obvious that Dallas and Houston would not be the best combination for the South and Southwest, it is not apparent whether the combination of Memphis and Miami, for example, is better than the combination of Dallas and Richmond.

Although "dealing out a full deck" with CASH ALPHA does not insure an absolutely best solution for the siting of a firm's lock-boxes, it does provide some narrowing of the field which can then be used to determine which combinations might be economically attractive. This might have been useful in the Ancama example. Ancama tested the inclusion of Atlanta against the whole system as it had existed prior to the test, and, under certain circumstances, Ancama might have added GF and eliminated its connection with 2D. But it might have been better for Ancama to have had a Miami bank and a North Carolina bank instead of an Atlanta bank. If Ancama tests for the addition of either the Miami bank or the North Carolina bank *after* it has already added Atlanta, then it will probably never be economic to add lock-box banks in these cities. Although "dealing out a full deck" would not necessarily show the combination of North Carolina and Miami as optimum, it should indicate that this combination might be a good solution.

4.5. Who Does the Analysis?

Many leading commercial banks advise their customers on how best to site lock-box banks. Some have the capacity, in terms of equipment, mail time and in-transit time data, and OR staff to provide customers with expert advice (of the generalized, Levy type) on lock-box siting. But unless a company is willing to confide in one bank the policy positions it has with its other banks, then analysis of the CASH ALPHA type must be done by the company or by an independent consultant in whom the company is willing to confide. This tends to leave the banks in the position of providing data on mail times and in-transit times (and on its own credit/charge schedule) but of *not* providing analysis of the customer's problem.

CASH ALPHA is probably of value to only a relatively small group of American industrial, utility, mercantile, and insurance firms that have major retail lock-box systems. These firms probably have their own computer equipment and people knowledgeable in linear programming formulation who, when working in conjunction with financial management, can duplicate CASH ALPHA.

For a firm the size of Ancama, CASH ALPHA could be run on an IBM 1410, 7040/44, 7090/94, 360 Model 30 or larger, a Univac 1107/1108, a CDC 1604 or 3600, or similar equipment. As the IBM 7090/94 can work with a linear programming formulation of slightly over 1,000 equations, the Ancama example (230 equations) is easily handled on this computer. It seems to me that the firms that could make use of CASH ALPHA will probably have available to them computers of at least this size, so that they could run CASH ALPHA without the necessity for decomposition of the model.

4.6. Other Thoughts on Ancama Corporation

The Ancama example is not a complete case study. There are other refinements that could be made. The wholesale lock-box system is perhaps the most obvious one. Care would have to be used in translating the retail lock-box experience to the wholesale lock-box area. Wholesale buyers simply do not pay their bills to the designated lock-box bank with the same regularity as do retail customers. Moreover, usually more wholesale items must be referred by a lock-box bank to its customer than is the case with the typical retail lock-box. A more sophisticated payroll system might also be introduced, so that payroll disbursements would form an independent variable just as general disbursements do.

I have left open the whole question of seasonality. In many cases, it may be well to run each CASH ALPHA test on the basis of a simulated year of twelve months rather than on the basis of a typical month.

It should be apparent that there is value in saving old data. If a company introduced CASH ALPHA, it would find value, I am sure, in saving the tapes that reflect actual results for each month so as to be able to test policy changes. With the most recent year's data on tape, for example, it would be easier to answer the question, "Well, if we *had* changed our policy as you suggest, what would have happened?"

Finally, although the prices of bank services have been assumed to be constant in this study, they obviously do change. The company using CASH ALPHA will be able to react to a price rise by agreeing or disagreeing, but it will also be able to make a "fine tuning" of its system by shifting a portion of its business to adjust for such a rise. If, in the Ancama example, 3B raised the price of each RLB item processed from 3¢ to 3.25¢, we should expect CASH ALPHA to reallocate RLB in the system so that 3B would still continue to get $150,000 in NCB. As a result, the total (as opposed to unit) cost of RLB at 3B would probably be kept constant. Cost of RLB at 3B in Alternate 4 had been 6,129 items at 3¢, or $183.87. We should expect that RLB volume would now go to ($183.87/0.0325) or 5,658 with the additional 471 items routed to Philadelphia, where the cost would be lower. The effect of the price increase on 3B would thus be a decrease in the work involved in handling these 471 items, *not* an increase in balances or revenues to the bank.

5 COMMENTS AND CONCLUSIONS

5.1. CASH ALPHA and Cash Administration

My main purpose in this study has been to discuss at some length a linear program approach to the structure of a firm's banking relations. But CASH ALPHA also has value in an ongoing situation because of the report-writing capability that its input and output provide. This section will cover briefly some of my thoughts on the use of CASH ALPHA in an ongoing cash administration system.

5.2. Periodic Forecasts

I see CASH ALPHA as a valuable monthly forecaster. Late in a month a firm might forecast all those factors that vary from month to month in the system. In the Ancama example, the Chicago Accounting Center might furnish for a coming month the data given in Table 5.1. This is the extent of

**Table 5.1. Chicago Accounting Center CASH ALPHA Input Data for
_____ , 1967**

CADIS	$9,415,000.00
CHRLB	105,500 items
CHCXD	750 items
CHLNS	$ 333,333.33
CH federal funds rate	4.25 per cent
CH 180-day C.D. rate	5.00 per cent
CHWLB	5,250 items
GFRLB	20,000 items
GFMUC	$ 38.52
LSDEP	$6,050,000.00
LSLNS	$ 333,333.33
LSMUC	$ 15.18
LSPAY	$4,355,250.00
LSWLB	8,000 items

68

needed input. Anything that has not changed since the prior running of the CASH ALPHA model need not be furnished. In addition to new forecasts, any change of terms would cause a change in the CASH ALPHA coefficients. For example, based on the new 5.00 per cent C.D. rate, CHVNB would now equal (0.05) (0.835) (30/360) CHNCB, or 0.003479 CHNCB, instead of the 0.003566 CHNCB used in the Ancama example for a typical month.

Accounting center data would be integrated at headquarters with head-quarters disbursement data and tax payment figures. The CASH ALPHA program would then be run, and accounting centers would be advised of the solution output. Chicago Accounting Center, for example, might receive the output cited in Table 5.2.

Table 5.2. Allocation of Business for _____, 1967 for Chicago Accounting Center

2YDIS	$6,687,604.75
CHDIS	564,084.74
GFDIS	965,752.14
LSDIS	1,197,558.37
	$9,415,000.00
CHFEE	$ 154.84
GFFEE	651.91
2YBAL	–
CHBAL	$ 813,751.39
GFBAL	–
LSBAL	–
2DTAX	$ 209,416.83
3STAX	200,000.00
CHTAX	511,505.72

The DIS and BAL information is needed for planning the month's activity. The FEE and TAX figures are for information only at this point. Taxes might more conveniently be paid by headquarters via wire transfer than by account-ing centers, and fees might be paid when billed by each bank. I envision that the first run of CASH ALPHA would be made just before the end of the month, prior to the receipt of fee and makeup cost data. This is a good time for a first run, I think, because the first tax payments during the coming month are payable on the first business day of the month.

The BAL information tells the accounting center where to peg its cash ledger average balances. For example, balances at CH would be held to an average of about $813,751.39. At the other Chicago Accounting Center banks, book balances would be held to zero. A way to accomplish this is to transfer funds daily to these banks, and then to disburse on the same day the amount that has been wired in. An approximately equal amount might be transferred each day to these banks with a zero book balance; with disbursements equaling the transfers in to the greatest extent possible, or transfers might be made on the basis of every other day, or every three days for each of the smaller disbursement banks. Care would have to be exercised to avoid making all payments on one bank so that a disproportionate amount of weekend float resulted there. There is a problem of balancing the operational simplicity of changing checks against the systems savings made possible by CASH ALPHA. A practice of making all the disbursements predicted for the month on one bank early in the month, and then shifting to another bank, should be avoided, because of the possibility that float would not always cover in-transit items and because of the limitations on flexibility that such an approach would create later on in the month.

It seems to me that it would be wise to rerun CASH ALPHA at midmonth, particularly if some banks allowed service-charge credit on the basis of actual days' usage of tax payments. The midmonth run could treat the credit value of the first of the month's tax payments as service-charge credits, or "MUK," and include as constraints the business that has actually been routed through a bank during a given month. For example, if disbursements for a given bank during the first half of a month had been $560,000, then at midmonth a new constraint calling for DIS at that bank to be equal to or in excess of $560,000 would be required to insure that the midmonth solution was feasible. More-over, if "BAL" had averaged $100,000 during the first half of the month, then in the new run BAL would have to be constrained at a level equal to or greater than $50,000, which would be the lowest average for the month without company ledger balances dropping below zero.

Other runs might be necessary. For example, let us assume that a major increase from the predicted disbursement level becomes known, due to a decision by the purchasing department to make extra large cash purchases of a raw material temporarily available at a bargain price. It would not necessarily be obvious where the float from the additional disbursements caused by the special purchase program could best be used. However, cost ranging of the CASH ALPHA solution in effect before the special purchase decision would indicate whether a change in solution was required for optimality. Then, if required, a new solution could be run. Experience may be helpful in indicating how often a firm may want to rerun CASH ALPHA. I think that two runs a month should suffice for most firms.

An end-of-month run of the CASH ALPHA model, based on exact knowledge of the CASH ALPHA input variables, might be useful in determining the cost of errors in forecasting. If the differences are significant, more attention could be focused on the prediction of important input variables such as RLB. The cost of additional forecasting effort should be measured against the results that better forecasting can be expected to provide. CASH ALPHA provides a mechanism for taking such a measure.

5.3. Management Reporting

Collection of actual data at the end of each month would not only facilitate rerunning of CASH ALPHA. It would also provide the input for electronic data processing report writing of information for use by financial management and also the data necessary for an updating of the coefficients used to predict the relationships between disbursements and balance levels. I have included as Appendixes F.1 through F.5 some forms that might be useful in managing an ongoing system. The reports facilitate management by exception, and they make available a good deal of data on the relative cost levels of the various banks. Although marginal costs are of prime value to the company in making spot decisions on where to do business, the competitive comparisons are of importance in determining where prices are out of line and, thus, where management action may be most effective.

Appendix F.5 fills a need for a comprehensive up-to-date summary of information relating to the dealings between the company and each of its banks, which is of great potential value in making maximum use of the relatively limited time that financial management can spend with its banks. A bank counterpart of this form might be most useful in keeping up-to-date on the total status of its dealings with major customers. The degree of elaborateness will vary from company to company. However, the adoption of CASH ALPHA in its planning function should carry "fallout" value in making comprehensive reports on the system trivial in cost.

5.4. Seasonality and CASH ALPHA

I have avoided the question of seasonality. It seems to me that it can be handled in a number of ways. If a company is on a flexible compensation basis with its banks, and if that system does not generate HQHQD or HQTAX — that is, unallocated headquarters disbursements or unallocated taxes during low activity months — then it may be worthwhile to ignore seasonality and let cash fees take up the extra high charges in peak activity months.

To predict what seasonality problems may exist, a firm might well run CASH ALPHA predictions for twelve months to see whether HQHQD or HQTAX show up. If they do, arrangements might be made with some banks in the system to calculate service-charge shortfall on an annual rather than on a monthly basis. This might be limited to a portion of the monthly shortfall.

For example, a bank might be willing to see service-charge shortfalls of $500 per month for three months during the year if the company made up the shortfall of $1,500 in three other months of the year by carrying sufficient additional NCB to earn service-charge credit of $1,500, calculated on the basis of a below-market service-charge credit rate on the additional NCB.

Even if no HQHQD or HQTAX results show up in any month, a more sophisticated version of CASH ALPHA is technically possible that bases all decisions on the best allocation of business during the present month *and* the next eleven months. The obvious potential advantage of this approach is that it would avoid the situation in which fees are the least expensive method of payment on a one-month basis but not the least expensive on a twelve-month moving average basis. A firm might arrange to make service-charge shortfalls on an annual basis with staggered close-out dates at the major banks. While some additional savings might be possible through this approach, it seems to me that the major value of CASH ALPHA would already have been achieved through its monthly use. Whatever additional value would accrue from the more elegant twelve-month model would have to be weighed against the additional forecasting burden this would place on the company.

5.5. Updating the Coefficients

One of the weakest areas in CASH ALPHA is the linkage between disbursements and float. Makeup cost provisions provide one way to handle errors in predicting float. Also, it is possible to update the model periodically, perhaps every six months, to take into account observed changes in the float coefficients.

But it may be possible to introduce a more sophisticated approach to coefficient updating with the capacity available in the newer generation of computers. There are undoubtedly long-term trends at work, as other firms introduce more sophisticated methods to expedite the collection of receipts. CASH ALPHA is hopefully one such example. And there are also seasonal trends at work, giving rise to greater float on disbursements during December when the postal system is flooded with Christmas mail than during other months of the year. Holidays in other months will also affect the mails and thus the generation of float. Exponential smoothing of actual monthly float factors would seem worthwhile. Alternatively, monthly coefficients might be calculated by regression analysis. Moreover, it should be technically possible to make the computer update coefficients constantly from information received by it on the generation of float. Daily statements furnished by the banks, when compared with disbursements, would enable the computer to keep up-to-date with respect to float coefficients.

Expansion of CASH ALPHA could take many forms. It is possible to envision on-line applications in which every decision made — that is, every check written — becomes input for all other decisions to be made in the system. An obvious integration possibility is with the short-term investment portfolio, discussed in the next section. CASH ALPHA is, I believe, a flexible vehicle for further experimentation, because no CASH ALPHA solution is ever out of touch with those policy decisions that are so important to good banking relations.

5.6. CASH ALPHA and the Short-Term Investment Portfolio

A simple example of the trade-off between compensating a bank for services rendered through the payment of cash fees and compensating it through added balances was discussed in Chapter 3, Section 3.3. But what if there are many banks that CASH ALPHA indicates should receive fees? Might not the company treasurer say, "O.K., we've structured our system on a 20 per cent pretax cost-of-capital basis. But now let's look at the coming month. I hate to see us invest in C.D.'s for the short run at 5 1/8 per cent if we could back out cash fees at the banks with balances, and perhaps increased receivables, at an implied rate higher than 5 1/8 per cent!" This is, to me, a reasonable position. The data that the treasurer needs can be provided by a PCR (profit cost ranging) computer run that focuses on cost-of-capital. Let us return to the optimal solution in Ancama's Alternate 4, the test of adding a new lock-box in Atlanta. The solution in that case was optimal provided that a 20 per cent pretax cost-of-capital was appropriate. What the computer now does is test to see how much this cost-of-capital could be lowered before a new solution would be required for optimality. When it reaches the point at which a new solution is required, the computer calculates and prints out a new solution. It then continues lowering the cost-of-capital, searching for "break" points, and solving and printing out solutions at each one. A PCR on cost-of-capital was run for Alternate 4, and a summary of the results of that run are included in Table 5.3. (The computer output for the PCR is too voluminous for inclusion in its entirety in this study; it consists of nine solution printouts and the iterations needed to reach each new solution from the prior solution.) If the proper trade-off is between C.D.'s and investment in company cash ledger balances and receivables, then the treasurer should select that PCR run based on a cost-of-capital rate that *just* exceeds the C.D. rate; in this case he would elect PCr run 6, the base allocation on a 6.35 per cent cost-of-capital basis. If the treasurer dropped to PCR run 7, he would be investing that increment of TOBAL + TORCV from PCR run 6 to PCR run 7 at 4.95 per cent rate — that is, investment in TOBAL + TORCV would have to go up by $83,796.75 (from $5,341,871.53 to $5,425,668.28) to wipe out the last $345.91 of cash fees, and the implicit yield of such a move is only 4.95 per cent: ($345.91)

(12)/$83,796.75 = 4.95 per cent. There is no "in between." In PCR run 6, the total cash fee of $345.91 is all paid to 2D. It is only when the cost of capital is lowered to 4.95 per cent that it is better to eliminate the 2DFEE with balances — at a cost of capital of 4.96 per cent, for example, the PCR run 6 solution is still the best. The treasurer will avoid investing that last $83,796.75 at 4.95 per cent when he can invest it at 5 1/8 per cent.

Table 5.3.   PCR on Cost-of-Capital, Ancama Alternate 4

Case	Pretax Cost-of-Capital (percentages)	TOBAL + TORCV	TOFEE
Alternate 4	20.00	$5,242,501.17	$1,124.93
PCR run 1	18.55	5,244.952.19	1,086.79
PCR run 2	11.68	5,260,003.06	934.46
PCR run 3	10.43	5,282,337.42	736.69
PCR run 4	9.16	5,304,890.78	558.52
PCR run 5	7.40	5,312,153.38	513.76
PCR run 6	6.35	5,341,871.53	345.91
PCR run 7	4.95	5,425,668.28	0
PCR run 8	0.61	5,556,226.90	0
PCR run 9	0	8,724,568.14	0

5.7.   Is It Practical?

The practicality of CASH ALPHA is a function of many independent variables. One is the cost of establishing and maintaining the system. A second is the availability of operations researchers — there is an opportunity cost for the operations research man's time as well as for the company's capital. A third is the attitude of the banks.

The first variable is relatively easy to answer. I purposely made Ancama's banking system "loose" in the sense that there are obvious ways of reducing the cost of the system. A great part of the value of CASH ALPHA is probably that it illustrates to financial management the potential value of a *systems view* of its banking relations. But beyond the systems view, the actual ability to calculate optimum allocations and to assist in system design, whether by "dealing off the top" or by "dealing out a full deck," should pay for the cost of CASH ALPHA many times over. Assuming that the firm makes short-term cash forecasts in any case for short-term financing decision purposes, there is little or no incremental time needed to adapt these forecasts to the CASH ALPHA input format. Thus the monthly cost of the system depends mainly on computer time used. A typical CASH ALPHA run for a firm the size of Ancama might require five minutes or less of IBM 7094 (or similar model) computer time and ten minutes or less of card read and print time. The total cost of a run should be $40 or less on an average cost basis, and obviously would be virtually nothing on a marginal cost basis for a firm with incremental machine time available. Key-punch time in an ongoing CASH ALPHA system would be trivial. *All* input costs could be more than offset by the CASH ALPHA EDP preparation of periodic management information reports, which could eliminate clerical time used in preparation of such reports.

The availability of people knowledgeable in linear program formulation is another factor that differs from one company to another. I suspect that the companies that have invested heavily in this kind of talent are in a better position to work with CASH ALPHA than are firms with little such investment. Consultants may be of value here, although this would depend on how willing a company was to disclose its policy positions to them.

The attitude of the banks is the most difficult to assess. The banks that are most concerned here are the relatively small number in the major banking center cities which compete for the large data-handling jobs associated with major industrial, utility, commercial, and finance firms. As is undoubtedly the case in industry, some of these banks are very rapidly adding operations research capabilities and integrating these capabilities into the management of the bank, and others are lagging. I believe that those banks that adopt the operations research outlook themselves cannot long resist their customers who take the same approach, even if it is tempting to do so in the short run. These banks will, I believe, lead in a pattern of increasing flexibility in terms of compensation for bank services.

The adoption of a management science approach by both banks and their major customers should not result in a decrease in quality of those services that the banks can provide for their customers at a lower cost or more effectively than the customers can themselves. A propensity to play safe for credit-reserve reasons should mean the continued existence of large demand deposits, even in the accounts of CASH ALPHA companies. They will want the ability to borrow on a large scale when the need arises, and their deposit balances in the meantime will pay for a good deal of intangibles. The only time CASH ALPHA should drive out compensation for intangible services is when the customer, after deliberation, decides that it wants neither the particular intangible service nor a call on that service. Assuming that the people who make these decisions are not shortsighted, the services that are driven out *should* be driven out. If the financial managers are shortsighted, they will make poor decisions without the benefit of CASH ALPHA! The question of the value of intangible services, in my opinion, should be as open to discussion as is the interest rate on a loan.

Ancama Corporation
Summary of Activity - Before CASH ALPHA

	(1) Co. Ledger Balance ($K)	(2) Plus: Float Gen. by Disbursing ($K)	(3) Gr. Bank Ledger Balance ($K)	(4) Less: Checks In Transit ($K)	(5) Net Collected Balance ($K)	(6) Avg. Monthly Tax Payments ($K)	(7) Monthly Value of Tangible Services 1/	(8) Tangible Services 2/	(9) Intangible Services
Second National Bank, New York	2 300	860	3 160	--	3 160	1 000	$ 260.00 4/	$ 260.00	$ 6 500.00
Wall Street Trust Company, New York	3 785	1 230	5 015	818	4 197	1 378	285.75 4/	285.75	7 000.00
Merchants National Bank, New York	1 000	1 150	2 150	--	2 150	1 000	2 133.50 4/	2 133.50	1 000.00
National Bank of Chicago	503	827	1 330	371	959	---	3 268.00	3 268.00	833.00
LaSalle Street Trust Company, Chicago	100	1 196	1 296	348	948	---	872.70	1 188.05	541.00
3rd National Bank of South Bend	250	--	250	--	250	---	.75 4/	.75	200.00
Second National Bank of Dallas	345	610	955	106	849	---	2 105.30	1 699.15	3/
3rd National Bank of Boston	946	241	1 187	62	1 125	---	2 080.20	1 592.50	833.00
Williams Trust Company, Boston	150	243	393	184	209	---	539.41	537.20	150.00
Philadelphia Trust Company	271	107	378	53	325	---	919.40	983.60	3/
Elm Street Trust Company, New Haven	150	--	150	--	150	---	1.00 4/	1.00	3/
U.S. National Bank of California	--	841	841	225	616	625	2 336.12	2 548.40	333.00
Union Trust Company, Los Angeles	184	350	534	184	350	---	416.18	427.93	1 666.00
Los Angeles Trust Company	--	267	267	--	267	---	95.70 4/	95.70	--
Sunnyville Trust Company	100	--	100	--	100	---	.85 4/	.85	3/
Total	10 084	7 922	18 006	2 351	15 655	4 003	$15 314.86	$15 022.38	$19 056.00

Footnotes:　1- Based on per item prices of individual banks (or on CH per item prices
　　　　　　　if no analysis statement requested)
　　　　　　2- Based on per item prices of National Bank of Chicago
　　　　　　3- Not quantified
　　　　　　4- Account analysis not requested - CH per item prices used

Cost of system to Ancama:
　@ 20% cost-of-capital:　monthly cost = ($10,084K)(.016667) = $168,070.03
　@ 6% cost-of-money:　monthly cost = ($10,084K)(.005) = $50,420.00

76

ACCOUNTING CENTER AND BANK SUMMARIES

New York Headquarters Activity
Monthly   - $K

	2nd Nat'l Bank	Merchants Nat'l Bank	Wall Street Trust	Total
Receipts				
Wholesale & Other	4 000	4 000	6 800	14 800
Net Transfers in From Field Banks 1/	1 285	2 196	1 246	4 727
Total	5 285	6 196	8 046	19 527
Disbursements				
General disbursements	3 150	5 800	5 700	14 650
Payroll	--	--	600	600
Ancama International	--	--	390	390
Dividends	750	--	--	750

Cash flow from operations   3 137
Less: Federal tax payments 2/   4 003
Total shortfall - met by net portfolio liquidations and borrowings   (766)

1/ Net transfers in

National Bank of Chicago	3 078		
LaSalle Street Trust Company	(860)		
2nd Nat'l Bank of Dallas	(931)		
3rd Nat'l Bank of So. Bend	(2)		
3rd Nat'l Bank of Boston		570	
Williams Trust Company		1 230	
Philadelphia Trust Company		397	
Elm Street Trust Company		(1)	
U.S. Nat'l Bank of California			745
Union Trust Company			2 005
Los Angeles Trust Company			(1 500)
Sunnyville Trust			(4)
	1 285	2 196	1 246

2/ Tax payments made by liquidating portfolio securities and wire transferring proceeds to selected banks. Wiring is done by one of the three New York banks, rotated monthly.

CASH ALPHA – BANK ACCOUNT SUMMARY

BANK Second National Bank	DATE ACCT. OPENED 1899	ADMINISTERED BY NYHQ
STREET ADDRESS	CITY, STATE & ZIP CODE	BANK TEL. NO.
101 Park Avenue, New York, N.Y. 10017		

OFFICERS & CONTACTS		BANK SIZE		
			AMOUNT (M Dollars)	STATUS 19 66 / 19 6
James E. Hauser	Chairman			
Wm. T. Carpenter	President			
Francis B. Donahue	Sr. VP	TOTAL DEPOSITS	10,426	
Herman Butler	VP (Branch Manager)	LOCAL CAPITAL	1,015	
Chas. W. Bradley	VP (Trust)	LOAN LIMIT	85	
William O. Branton	VP (International)	RANK BY SIZE · U.S.		3 / 3
Arnold G. Sims	AVP (Branch)	STATE		2 / 2
Leonard R. Vaughan	AVP (Branch)	CITY		2 / 2
		NO. OF BRANCHES		119 / 109

BANKING ACTIVITY (MONTHLY)

COMPANY UNIT	ACCOUNT TITLE	BALANCES (K$)		VOLUMES (K$)		NO. OF CHECKS		TRANSFERS (K$) TO (FROM)
		CO. LEDGER	BANK—NCB	DEPOSITS	PAYMENTS	DEPOSIT	PAYMENT	
Headquarters	Regular	2,300	2,970	4,000	3,150	–	1,250	(NB of Chi
	Dividend	–	190	–	750	–	3,730	LaSalle St.
								2NB–Dallas
								3NB–So.Bend
	Total	2,300	3,160	4,000	3,900	–	4,980	

MONTHLY ACCOUNT ANALYSIS

SERVICE CHARGE CREDITS LESS ACTIVITY CHARGES		COMPETITIVE BASIS	BANK BASIS	INCREMENTAL BASIS
AVG. DAILY BALANCES	COMPANY LEDGER	$ 2,300,000	Not requested	
	PLUS: FLOAT GENERATED BY DISBURSING	860,000		
GROSS BANK STATEMENT BALANCES		$ 3,160,000		
LESS: CHECKS IN TRANSIT		–		
NET COLLECTED BALANCE		$ 3,160,000		
LESS: FEDERAL RESERVE: 16½ %		521,400		
AVAILABLE FOR INVESTMENT		$ 2,638,600		
EARNINGS	ON AFI COMPETITIVE 5 %; BANK – %	$ 10,994.18		
	ON TAXES: COMPETITIVE 5 %; BANK – %	2,500.00	(4½% for 20 days on $1,000K)	
	TOTAL	$ 13,494.18		
LESS ACTIVITY CHARGES (DETAILED BELOW)		260.00		
SERVICE CHARGE CREDITS LESS ACTIVITY CHARGES		$ 13,234.18		

ACTIVITY CHARGES		ITEMS	RATE	PRICE	RATE	PRICE
CHECKS PAID		4,980	.05	249.00		
CHECKS DEPOSITED	REGULAR					
	RETAIL LOCK BOX					
	WHOLESALE LOCK BOX					
DEPOSIT TICKETS						
INTERBRANCH DEPOSITS						
TRANSFERS		9	1.00	9.00		
RETURNED CHECKS						
STOP PAYMENTS		2	1.00	2.00		
ACCOUNT RECONCILIATION						
TOTAL ACTIVITY CHARGES				260.00		

LOAN ACTIVITY

CO. UNIT BENEFITING	IDENTIFICATION	RATE	DATED	MATURITY	AMOUNT OF LOAN ORIGINAL	BALANCE	AS OF
ncama	Line of credit	Prime	-	-	$10,000,000	$ 5,000,000*	3/31/67
ncama Int'l.	10-year T/L	4-3/4-5%	2/1/62	2/1/72	2,000,000	1,400,000	"
ncama-Ajax	Term Loan	4-3/4%	12/1/63	12/1/68	1,000,000	700,000*	"
	* 6-month moving average of usage						

AGREEMENT ON COMPENSATING BALANCE   No agreement.

POLICY CONSTRAINTS   Minimum average NCB of 15% of outstanding loans plus 10% of unused lines plus $1,000,000. Also, minimum average NCB not to fall below $3.1 million on a 6-month moving average basis.

VALUE OF INTANGIBLE SERVICES			
	PER MONTH	PER YEAR	COMMENT
GENERAL ADVISORY	$ 4,167.	$ 20,000.	
INTERNATIONAL	1,667.	50,000.	
NEW BUSINESS			
MERGERS & ACQUISITIONS			
CREDIT INFORMATION	667.	8,000.	
TOTAL	$ 6,500.	$ 78,000.	

REMARKS: This bank has always been agent bank on the company's major syndicated credits. It has not been as aggressive as Wall Street Trust for additional business. We have told the bank that one result of the present banking study is that Second National will see a sharp reduction in tax payments. This announcement caused no appreciable reaction; however, the bank did state emphatically that they hoped we would not be cutting balances.

LONG RANGE PLANS
See POLICY CONSTRAINTS

CASH ALPHA – BANK ACCOUNT SUMMARY

BANK	DATE ACCT. OPENED	ADMINISTERED BY
Wall Street Trust Company	1914	NYHQ

STREET ADDRESS	CITY, STATE & ZIP CODE	BANK TEL. NO.
555 Wall Street	New York, New York 10015	

OFFICERS & CONTACTS		BANK SIZE		
			AMOUNT (M Dollars)	STATUS 1966 / 19 6
Michael J. Johnson	Chairman			
Edward L. Parks	President			
John P. Hines	Exec. VP	TOTAL DEPOSITS	10,425	
Paul E. Daniels	VP (Branch Manager)	LOCAL CAPITAL	1,216	
Albert O. Dana	VP (Branch)	LOAN LIMIT	90	
Mitchell W. Cooper	AVP (Branch)	RANK BY SIZE — U.S.		4 / 4
Harold Rubin	AVP (Branch)	RANK BY SIZE — STATE		3 / 3
		RANK BY SIZE — CITY		3 / 3
		NO. OF BRANCHES		181 / 170

BANKING ACTIVITY (MONTHLY)

COMPANY UNIT	ACCOUNT TITLE	BALANCES (K$)		VOLUMES (K$)		NO. OF CHECKS		TRANSFERS (K$) TO (FROM)
		CO. LEDGER	BANK–NCB	DEPOSITS	PAYMENTS	DEPOSIT	PAYMENT	
Headquarters	Regular	3,685	3,882	6,800	5,700	2,800	1,275	(3N/B–Bos)
	Payroll	–	65	–	600	–	1,200	Williams TC
Ancama Int'l	Regular	100	250	–	390	300	800	(Phila TC)
								Elm St. TC
Total		3,785	4,197	6,800	6,690	3,100	3,275	

MONTHLY ACCOUNT ANALYSIS

SERVICE CHARGE CREDITS LESS ACTIVITY CHARGES		COMPETITIVE BASIS	BANK BASIS	INCREMENTAL BASIS
AVG. DAILY BALANCES	COMPANY LEDGER	$3,785,000	Not requested	
	PLUS: FLOAT GENERATED BY DISBURSING	1,230,000		
GROSS BANK STATEMENT BALANCES		$5,015,000		
LESS: CHECKS IN TRANSIT		818,000		
NET COLLECTED BALANCE		$4,197,000		
LESS: FEDERAL RESERVE: $16\frac{1}{2}$ %		692,505		
AVAILABLE FOR INVESTMENT		$3,504,495		
EARNINGS	ON AFI COMPETITIVE 5 %; BANK %	14,602.06		
	ON TAXES: COMPETITIVE %; BANK %	3,445.00	($4\frac{1}{2}$% for 20 days on $1,378K)	
	TOTAL	$ 18,047.06		
LESS ACTIVITY CHARGES (DETAILED BELOW)		285.75		
SERVICE CHARGE CREDITS LESS ACTIVITY CHARGES		$ 17,761.31		

ACTIVITY CHARGES		ITEMS	RATE	PRICE	RATE	PRICE	
CHECKS PAID		3,275	.05	163.75			
CHECKS DEPOSITED	REGULAR	3,100	.02	62.00			
	RETAIL LOCK BOX						
	WHOLESALE LOCK BOX						
DEPOSIT TICKETS		600	.05	30.00			
INTERBRANCH DEPOSITS							
TRANSFERS		30	1.00	30.00			
RETURNED CHECKS							
STOP PAYMENTS							
ACCOUNT RECONCILIATION							
TOTAL ACTIVITY CHARGES				285.75			

. UNIT EFITING	IDENTIFICATION	RATE	DATED	MATURITY	AMOUNT OF LOAN		AS OF
					ORIGINAL	BALANCE	
:ama	Line of credit	Prime			10,000,000	3,000,000*	3/31/67
:ama Int'l	10-year T/L	4-3/4 - 5%	2/1/62	2/1/72	4,000,000	2,800,000	
	* 6-month moving average of usage						

EEMENT ON COMPENSATING BALANCE   No agreement.

ICY CONSTRAINTS   Minimum average NCB of 15% of outstanding loans plus 10% of unused lines
plus $1,000,000. Also, minimum average NCB not to fall below $4.0 million
on a 6-month moving average basis.

VALUE OF INTANGIBLE SERVICES			
	PER MONTH	PER YEAR	COMMENT
ERAL ADVISORY	$ 2,500	$ 30,000	
RNATIONAL	4,167	50,000	
BUSINESS			
GERS & ACQUISITIONS			
DIT INFORMATION	333	4,000	
TOTAL	$ 7,000	$ 84,000	

ARKS: We told the bank that our revised cash movement system meant a decrease in tax payments.
We also indicated that we would make a quite small decrease in average balances. The bank
argues persuasively that they are constantly furnishing ideas of value for us, particularly in our international operations. Moreover, the bank says that it has always
wanted more of our loan activity than we would let it have, and that its willingness to
step up and take any reasonable loan amount, even in periods of tight money, has been
amply demonstrated in the past.

RANGE PLANS   See POLICY CONSTRAINTS.

CASH ALPHA – BANK ACCOUNT SUMMARY

BANK	DATE ACCT. OPENED	ADMINISTERED BY
Merchants National Bank	1949	NYHQ

STREET ADDRESS	CITY, STATE & ZIP CODE	BANK TEL. NO.
1313 Wall Street	New York, New York 10015	

OFFICERS & CONTACTS		BANK SIZE		
			AMOUNT (M Dollars)	STATUS
				19 66 / 19
Marcus A. Hawkins	Chairman			
Anthony McMahon	President			
Sidney L. Silverman	Sr. VP	TOTAL DEPOSITS	4,181	
Harold A. Walters	VP	LOCAL CAPITAL	501	
Michael B. Kelly	VP	LOAN LIMIT	50	
		RANK BY SIZE — U.S.		10 / 1
		STATE		4
		CITY		4
		NO. OF BRANCHES		126 / 10

BANKING ACTIVITY (MONTHLY)

COMPANY UNIT	ACCOUNT TITLE	BALANCES (K$)		VOLUMES (K$)		NO. OF CHECKS		TRANSFERS (K$) TO (FROM)
		CO. LEDGER	BANK–NCB	DEPOSITS	PAYMENTS	DEPOSIT	PAYMENT	
Headquarters	Regular	1,000	2,150	4,000	5,800	–	2,450	(USNB CAL)
								(Union TC)
								LA TC
								Sunnyville
Total		1,000	2,150	4,000	5,800	–	2,450	

MONTHLY ACCOUNT ANALYSIS

SERVICE CHARGE CREDITS LESS ACTIVITY CHARGES		COMPETITIVE BASIS	BANK BASIS	INCREMENTAL BASIS
AVG. DAILY BALANCES	COMPANY LEDGER	$ 1,000,000	Not requested	
	PLUS: FLOAT GENERATED BY DISBURSING	1,150,000		
GROSS BANK STATEMENT BALANCES		$ 2,150,000		
LESS: CHECKS IN TRANSIT		–		
NET COLLECTED BALANCE		$ 2,150,000		
LESS: FEDERAL RESERVE: 16½ %		354,750		
AVAILABLE FOR INVESTMENT		$ 1,795,250		
EARNINGS	ON APT COMPETITIVE 5 %; BANK %	$ 7,480.21		
	ON TAXES: COMPETITIVE %; BANK %	2,500.00	(4½% for 20 days on $1,000K	
	TOTAL	$ 9,980.21		
LESS ACTIVITY CHARGES (DETAILED BELOW)		2,133.50		
SERVICE CHARGE CREDITS LESS ACTIVITY CHARGES		$ 7,846.71		

ACTIVITY CHARGES		ITEMS	RATE	PRICE	RATE	PRICE	
CHECKS PAID		2,450	.05	122.50			
CHECKS DEPOSITED	REGULAR						
	RETAIL LOCK BOX						
	WHOLESALE LOCK BOX						
DEPOSIT TICKETS							
INTERBRANCH DEPOSITS							
TRANSFERS		11	1.00	11.00			
RETURNED CHECKS							
STOP PAYMENTS							
ACCOUNT RECONCILIATION							
Receipt/Delivery/Custody of Securities				2000.00			
TOTAL ACTIVITY CHARGES				2133.50			

CO. UNIT BENEFITING	IDENTIFICATION	RATE	DATED	MATURITY	AMOUNT OF LOAN		
					ORIGINAL	BALANCE	AS OF
Ancama	Line of credit	Prime			5,000,000	2,000,000*	3/31/67
Ancama Int'l	10-year T/L	4-3/4%-5%	2/1/62	2/1/72	1,500,000	1,050,000	"
	* 6-month moving average of usage						

AGREEMENT ON COMPENSATING BALANCE   No agreement.

POLICY CONSTRAINTS   Minimum NCB of 15% of outstanding loans plus 10% of unused lines plus $1,000,000.

VALUE OF INTANGIBLE SERVICES			
	PER MONTH	PER YEAR	COMMENT
GENERAL ADVISORY	$ 1,000	$ 12,000	
INTERNATIONAL			
NEW BUSINESS			
MERGERS & ACQUISITIONS			
CREDIT INFORMATION			
TOTAL	$ 1,000	$ 12,000	

REMARKS: Despite this bank's evident desire to do more for Ancama, we invariably prefer to deal with Second National or Wall Street Trust. The bank knows this, and knows we plan to reduce our activity here, and reduce or eliminate tax payments.

Based on tangible and intangible services, we estimate that excess balances total some $1,550,000. On the compensating balance formula, balances are $392,000 too high if we look to Merchants for a potential additional $10 million, $892,000 too high if we look for $5 million. Although we would probably not look to Merchants for a full $10 million, we simply cannot eliminate all tax payments and reduce balances by close to $1 million at one time with this very important bank.

LONG RANGE PLANS

Major review in April '68.

Chicago Accounting Center Activity
Monthly - $K

Receipts	Nat'l Bank of Chicago	LaSalle St. Trust Co.	2nd Nat'l Bank of Dallas	3rd Nat'l Bank of So.Bend	Total
Retail lock-box	3 078	-	1 769	-	4 847
Wholesale lock-box	4 000	6 110	-	-	10 110
Over-the-counter	250	-	-	-	250
Total	7 328	6 110	1 769	-	15 207

Disbursements

	Nat'l Bank of Chicago	LaSalle St. Trust Co.	2nd Nat'l Bank of Dallas	3rd Nat'l Bank of So.Bend	Total
General disbursements	4 250	2 650	2 700	2	9 602
Payroll	-	4 320	-	-	4 320
Total	4 250	6 970	2 700	2	13 922

	Nat'l Bank of Chicago	LaSalle St. Trust Co.	2nd Nat'l Bank of Dallas	3rd Nat'l Bank of So.Bend	Total
Net transfer to (from) Headquarters	3 078	(860)	(931)	(2)	1 285

BANK	National Bank of Chicago		DATE ACCT. OPENED 1929	ADMINISTERED BY Chicago Acctg. Center

STREET ADDRESS 1401 La Salle Street	CITY, STATE & ZIP CODE Chicago, Illinois 60690	BANK TEL. NO.

OFFICERS & CONTACTS		BANK SIZE		
Wm. P. Denton	Chairman		AMOUNT (M Dollars)	STATUS 19 66	65
Peter J. Petersen	President			
George T. Rodgers	Sr. VP	TOTAL DEPOSITS	5,109	
Alan O. Harris	VP	LOCAL CAPITAL	656	
Murphy M. Michaels	VP	LOAN LIMIT	45	
Joseph B. Alwood	VP	RANK BY SIZE — U.S.		6	7
		STATE		1	2
		CITY		1	2
		NO. OF BRANCHES		0	0

BANKING ACTIVITY (MONTHLY)

COMPANY UNIT	ACCOUNT TITLE	BALANCES (K$)		VOLUMES (K$)		NO. OF CHECKS		TRANSFERS (K$) TO (FROM)
		CO. LEDGER	BANK–NCB	DEPOSITS	PAYMENTS	DEPOSIT	PAYMENT	
Chicago A/C	Regular	503	959	250	4,250	700	1,900	LSSTC-Chi.
	Retail L/B	–	–	3,078		73,000		2NB-NYC
	Wholesale L/B	–	–	4,000		5,100		
	Total	503	959	7,328	4,250	78,800	1,900	

MONTHLY ACCOUNT ANALYSIS

SERVICE CHARGE CREDITS LESS ACTIVITY CHARGES		COMPETITIVE BASIS	BANK BASIS	INCREMENTAL BASIS
AVG. DAILY BALANCES	COMPANY LEDGER	CH is the	$ 503,000	
	PLUS: FLOAT GENERATED BY DISBURSING	basis for	827,000	
GROSS BANK STATEMENT BALANCES		"competitive	$1,330,000	
LESS: CHECKS IN TRANSIT		basis"	371,000	
NET COLLECTED BALANCE			$ 959,000	
LESS: FEDERAL RESERVE: $16\frac{1}{2}$ %			158,235	
AVAILABLE FOR INVESTMENT			$ 800,765	
EARNINGS	ON AFT COMPETITIVE %; BANK 5 %		3,336.52	
	ON TAXES: COMPETITIVE %; BANK %		–	
	TOTAL		3,336.52	$ 3,336.52
LESS ACTIVITY CHARGES (DETAILED BELOW)			3,268.00	$ 2,435.00
SERVICE CHARGE CREDITS LESS ACTIVITY CHARGES			68.52	$ 901.52

ACTIVITY CHARGES		ITEMS	RATE	PRICE	RATE	PRICE	
CHECKS PAID		1,900	Same as		.05	$ 95.00	Employees:
CHECKS DEPOSITED	REGULAR	700	bank basis		.02	14.00	
	RETAIL LOCK BOX	73,000			.0375	2737.50	3 @ $500-$1500
	WHOLESALE LOCK BOX	5,100			.065	331.50	1 @ 500- 500
DEPOSIT TICKETS							1/2 @ 800- 400
INTERBRANCH DEPOSITS							
TRANSFERS		30			1.00	30.00	
RETURNED CHECKS							
STOP PAYMENTS							
ACCOUNT RECONCILIATION					Flat	25.00	
Postage						35.00	35
TOTAL ACTIVITY CHARGES						$3268.00	$2435.

CO. UNIT BENEFITING	IDENTIFICATION	RATE	DATED	MATURITY	AMOUNT OF LOAN		
					ORIGINAL	BALANCE	AS OF
Ancama Int'l.	10-year T/L	4-3/4%-5%	2/1/62	1/31/72	$ 500,000	$ 350,000	3/31/6

AGREEMENT ON COMPENSATING BALANCE   No agreement.

POLICY CONSTRAINTS   Minimum NCB of 15% of outstanding loans plus $500,000.

VALUE OF INTANGIBLE SERVICES			
	PER MONTH	PER YEAR	COMMENT
GENERAL ADVISORY	$ 500	$ 6,000	
INTERNATIONAL			
NEW BUSINESS			
MERGERS & ACQUISITIONS			
CREDIT INFORMATION	333	4,000	
TOTAL	$ 833	$ 10,000	

REMARKS: Agreement reach January '67:

(1) Schedule of service charges unchanged.
(2) Service charge credit to be allowed on AFI at rate paid on 180-day C/Ds.
(3) Service charge credit on tax payments...20 days at 1/4% below the current
    Fed. Funds rate, minimum 2.5%.
(4) Credit for tax payments not to exceed 1/3 of total service charge credit.
(5) Agrees to cash fee for service charge shortfall, but not to exceed 1/3 of
    total service charge credit.
(6) NCB to average at least $500,000 (but see policy statement above - bank does
    not know of our policy position).
(7) Trial period for one year, to 3/31/68, then subject to review.

LONG RANGE PLANS
      This bank will continue to be one of Ancama's two major Midwestern banks.

86

CASH ALPHA – BANK ACCOUNT SUMMARY

Appendix B7

.NK La Salle Street Trust Company	DATE ACCT. OPENED 1947	ADMINISTERED BY Chicago Acctg. Center
REET ADDRESS 2323 La Salle Street	CITY, STATE & ZIP CODE Chicago, Illinois 60690	BANK TEL. NO.

OFFICERS & CONTACTS		BANK SIZE			
			AMOUNT (M Dollars)	STATUS 1966	1965
Louis M. Earl	Chairman				
Joseph K. Leonard	President				
Samuel B. Fox	Exec. VP	TOTAL DEPOSITS	5,108		
Max T. Starr	VP	LOCAL CAPITAL	655		
John M. Llewellyn	VP	LOAN LIMIT	45		
		RANK BY SIZE — U.S.		7	6
		STATE		2	1
		CITY		2	1
		NO. OF BRANCHES		0	0

BANKING ACTIVITY (MONTHLY)

COMPANY UNIT	ACCOUNT TITLE	BALANCES (K$)		VOLUMES (K$)		NO. OF CHECKS		TRANSFERS (K$) TO (FROM)
		CO. LEDGER	BANK–NCB	DEPOSITS	PAYMENTS	DEPOSIT	PAYMENT	
Chicago A/C	Regular	100	292	–	2,650	–	1,900	(NB of Chi)
	Payroll	–	656	–	4,320	–	8,900	(2NB-NYC)
	Wholesale L/B	–	–	6,110	–	7,900	–	
	Total	100	948	6,110	6,970	7,900	10,800	

MONTHLY ACCOUNT ANALYSIS

SERVICE CHARGE CREDITS LESS ACTIVITY CHARGES		COMPETITIVE BASIS	BANK BASIS	INCREMENTAL BASIS
AVG. DAILY BALANCES	COMPANY LEDGER	$ 100,000	$ 100,000	
	PLUS: FLOAT GENERATED BY DISBURSING	1,196,000	1,196,000	
GROSS BANK STATEMENT BALANCES		$ 1,296,000	$ 1,296,000	
LESS: CHECKS IN TRANSIT		348,000	348,000	
NET COLLECTED BALANCE		$ 948,000	$ 948,000	
LESS: FEDERAL RESERVE: 16½ %		156,420	156,420	
AVAILABLE FOR INVESTMENT		791,580	791,580	
EARNINGS	ON AFL: COMPETITIVE 5 %; BANK 2½ %	$ 3,298.25	$ 1,649.13	
	ON TAXES: COMPETITIVE % ; BANK %			
	TOTAL	$ 3,298.25	$ 1,649.13	$ 3,271.86
LESS ACTIVITY CHARGES (DETAILED BELOW)		$ 1,188.05	$ 872.70	700.00
SERVICE CHARGE CREDITS LESS ACTIVITY CHARGES		$ 2,110.20	$ 776.43	$ 2,571.86

ACTIVITY CHARGES		ITEMS	RATE	PRICE	RATE	PRICE		
CHECKS PAID		10,800	.05	$540.00	.035	$378.00		
CHECKS DEPOSITED	REGULAR							
	RETAIL LOCK BOX							
	WHOLESALE LOCK BOX	7,900	.065	$513.50	.05	$395.00	1 @ 500	500
DEPOSIT TICKETS							1/4 @ 800	200
INTERBRANCH DEPOSITS								
TRANSFERS								
RETURNED CHECKS								
STOP PAYMENTS								
ACCOUNT RECONCILIATION		6,970	.015	$104.55	.01	$ 69.70		
Postage				30.00		30.00		
TOTAL ACTIVITY CHARGES				$1188.05		$872.70		$700

87

CO. UNIT BENEFITING	IDENTIFICATION	RATE	DATED	MATURITY	AMOUNT OF LOAN		
					ORIGINAL	BALANCE	AS OF
Ancama Int'l	10-year T/L	4-1/2-4-3/4%	2/1/62	1/31/72	500,000	350,000	3/31

AGREEMENT ON COMPENSATING BALANCE   No agreement.

POLICY CONSTRAINTS   Minimum NCB of 15% of outstanding loans plus $500,000.

VALUE OF INTANGIBLE SERVICES			
	PER MONTH	PER YEAR	COMMENT
GENERAL ADVISORY	$ 208	$ 2,500	
INTERNATIONAL			
NEW BUSINESS			
MERGERS & ACQUISITIONS			
CREDIT INFORMATION	$ 333	$ 4,000	
TOTAL	$ 541	$ 6,500	

REMARKS: Discussions in January '67:

(1) Agreed to increase service charge credit on NCB to 3%.
(2) Will not adjust costs.
(3) Service charge credit on tax payments ... 20 days at 2%.
(4) Expects 20% balances on loans (but see Policy above, which will be greater than 20% on the Ancama Int'l loan -- bank does not know of our policy posit
(5) Bank will not accept cash fees in lieu of balances.

LONG RANGE PLANS
Continue to use this bank for the major portion of wholesale lock box activity. But in view of attitude on costs, review possibility of major change in April '

88

CASH ALPHA – BANK ACCOUNT SUMMARY

ANK	DATE ACCT. OPENED	ADMINISTERED BY
Second National Bank of Dallas	1939	Chicago Acctg. Center

TREET ADDRESS	CITY, STATE & ZIP CODE	BANK TEL. NO.
10419 Akard Street	Dallas, Texas 75221	

OFFICERS & CONTACTS		BANK SIZE		
ade Smith	Chairman		AMOUNT (M Dollars)	STATUS
oseph A. Earnest	President			19 66 | 19 65
lfred O. Bolton	Sr. VP	TOTAL DEPOSITS	1,198	
harles E. Myers	Sr. VP	LOCAL CAPITAL	106	
.J. Alston	VP	LOAN LIMIT	10.4	
		RANK BY SIZE — U.S.		36 | 34
		STATE		3 | 3
		CITY		3 | 3
		NO. OF BRANCHES		0 | 0

BANKING ACTIVITY (MONTHLY)

COMPANY UNIT	ACCOUNT TITLE	BALANCES (K$)		VOLUMES (K$)		NO. OF CHECKS		TRANSFERS (K$) TO (FROM)
		CO. LEDGER	BANK–NCB	DEPOSITS	PAYMENTS	DEPOSIT	PAYMENT	
hicago A/C	Regular	345	849	–	2,700	–	1,160	(NB of Chi)
	Retail L/B	–	–	1,769	–	42,500	–	(2NB NYC)
	Total	345	849	1,769	2,700	42,500	1,160	

MONTHLY ACCOUNT ANALYSIS

SERVICE CHARGE CREDITS LESS ACTIVITY CHARGES		COMPETITIVE BASIS	BANK BASIS	INCREMENTAL BASIS
AVG. DAILY BALANCES	COMPANY LEDGER	$ 345,000	$ 345,000	
	PLUS: FLOAT GENERATED BY DISBURSING	610,000	610,000	
ROSS BANK STATEMENT BALANCES		$ 955,000	$ 955,000	
ESS: CHECKS IN TRANSIT		106,000	106,000	
ET COLLECTED BALANCE		$ 849,000	$ 849,000	
ESS: FEDERAL RESERVE: 16½ %		140,085	140,085	
VAILABLE FOR INVESTMENT		$ 708,915	$ 708,915	
EARNINGS	ON AFI COMPETITIVE 5 %; BANK 3.6 %	$ 2,953.81	$ 2,126.75	
	ON TAXES: COMPETITIVE %; BANK %	–	–	
	TOTAL	$ 2,953.81	$ 2,126.75	$ 2,953.81
SS ACTIVITY CHARGES (DETAILED BELOW)		1,669.15	2,105.30	1,250.00
RVICE CHARGE CREDITS LESS ACTIVITY CHARGES		$ 1,284.66	$ 21.45	$ 1,703.81

ACTIVITY CHARGES		ITEMS	RATE	PRICE	RATE	PRICE	
HECKS PAID		1,160	.05	58.00	.06	69.60	
CHECKS DEPOSITED	REGULAR						
	RETAIL LOCK BOX	42,500	.0375	1,593.75	.045	1,912.50	1.7 @ 500 850
	WHOLESALE LOCK BOX						1/2 @ 800 400
POSIT TICKETS							
TERBRANCH DEPOSITS							
ANSFERS							
TURNED CHECKS							
OP PAYMENTS							
COUNT RECONCILIATION		1,160	.015	17.40	.02	23.20	
anagement Fee						100.00	
TOTAL ACTIVITY CHARGES				1,669.15		2,105.30	1,250

CO. UNIT BENEFITING	IDENTIFICATION	RATE	DATED	MATURITY	AMOUNT OF LOAN		AS O
					ORIGINAL	BALANCE	
	None						

AGREEMENT ON COMPENSATING BALANCE

POLICY CONSTRAINTS

VALUE OF INTANGIBLE SERVICES			
	PER MONTH	PER YEAR	COMMENT
GENERAL ADVISORY			
INTERNATIONAL			
NEW BUSINESS	$ 200	$ 2,400	
MERGERS & ACQUISITIONS			
CREDIT INFORMATION			
TOTAL	$ 200	$ 2,400	

REMARKS:
After prolonged discussion late last year, the Second reluctantly agreed to cut the lock box charge to 4½¢ per item from 5½¢. However, the bank was unwilling to remove the long-disputed monthly overhead fee, or to adjust the earnings rate upward. The 1 change in the lock box charge enabled us to reduce balances by approximately $175,000 to the present level. Because we have just completed these discussions, the time is not ripe for intensive new discussions.

This has been Ancama's major bank in the Southwest for many years, and every effort should be made to work out an economical arrangement with it. However, this bank's high costs make it a candidate for elimination/major adjustment analysis after CASH ALPHA's first year of operation.

LONG RANGE PLANS
Major analysis in April '68. No change until then.

NK	DATE ACCT. OPENED	ADMINISTERED BY
3rd National Bank of South Bend	1924	Chicago Acctg. Center
REET ADDRESS	CITY, STATE & ZIP CODE	BANK TEL. NO.
971 Main Street	South Bend, Indiana	

OFFICERS & CONTACTS		BANK SIZE		
eorge T. Morris	Chairman		AMOUNT (M Dollars)	STATUS
amuel R. Leonard	President			1966 / 1965
enjamin K. Bell	Sr. VP	TOTAL DEPOSITS	78	
ouis A. Masters	VP	LOCAL CAPITAL	7.4	
		LOAN LIMIT	.7	
		RANK BY SIZE — U.S.		484 / 462
		STATE	5 / 5	
		CITY	1 / 1	
		NO. OF BRANCHES	19 / 17	

BANKING ACTIVITY (MONTHLY)

COMPANY UNIT	ACCOUNT TITLE	BALANCES (K$)		VOLUMES (K$)		NO. OF CHECKS		TRANSFERS (K$) TO (FROM)
		CO. LEDGER	BANK–NCB	DEPOSITS	PAYMENTS	DEPOSIT	PAYMENT	
hicago A/C	Regular	225	225	-	-	-	-	(NB of Chi)
	Emergency	25	25	-	2	-	15	(2NB NYC)
	Total	250	250	-	2	-	15	

MONTHLY ACCOUNT ANALYSIS

SERVICE CHARGE CREDITS LESS ACTIVITY CHARGES		COMPETITIVE BASIS	BANK BASIS	INCREMENTAL BASIS
AVG. DAILY BALANCES	COMPANY LEDGER	$ 250,000	Not requested	
	PLUS: FLOAT GENERATED BY DISBURSING	-		
GROSS BANK STATEMENT BALANCES		$ 250,000		
LESS: CHECKS IN TRANSIT		-		
NET COLLECTED BALANCE		$ 250,000		
LESS: FEDERAL RESERVE: 16½ %		41,250		
AVAILABLE FOR INVESTMENT		$ 208,750		
EARNINGS	ON AFI COMPETITIVE 5 %; BANK %	$ 869.79		
	ON TAXES: COMPETITIVE %; BANK %	-		
	TOTAL	$ 869.79		
LESS ACTIVITY CHARGES (DETAILED BELOW)		.75		
SERVICE CHARGE CREDITS LESS ACTIVITY CHARGES		$ 869.04		

ACTIVITY CHARGES		ITEMS	RATE	PRICE	RATE	PRICE	
CHECKS PAID		15	.05	.75			
CHECKS DEPOSITED	REGULAR						
	RETAIL LOCK BOX						
	WHOLESALE LOCK BOX						
DEPOSIT TICKETS							
INTERBRANCH DEPOSITS							
TRANSFERS							
RETURNED CHECKS							
STOP PAYMENTS							
ACCOUNT RECONCILIATION							
TOTAL ACTIVITY CHARGES				.75			

| CO. UNIT BENEFITING | IDENTIFICATION | RATE | DATED | MATURITY | AMOUNT OF LOAN | | |
					ORIGINAL	BALANCE	AS
None							

AGREEMENT ON COMPENSATING BALANCE

POLICY CONSTRAINTS   See remarks.

VALUE OF INTANGIBLE SERVICES			
	PER MONTH	PER YEAR	COMMENT
GENERAL ADVISORY			
INTERNATIONAL			
NEW BUSINESS			
MERGERS & ACQUISITIONS			
CREDIT INFORMATION			
TOTAL			

REMARKS: When disbursing was moved out of the South Bend plant and into the Chicago Accounting Center, it was decided to maintain a substantial bank balance with the 3rd National, even though its check processing services were no longer required.

It is difficult to quantify the annual value of this relationship. However, at the time of the consolidation of accounting functions in Chicago, all were agreed that total balances of $250,000 (the plant manager's $25,000 emergency fund and $225,000 fixed balance in the regular account) were about right. The bank, while unhappy at the news of the consolidation, was very appreciative of our willingness to keep substantial balances there. No major change is in order now.

LONG RANGE PLANS   No change.

Boston Accounting Center Activity
Monthly - $K

Receipts	3rd Nat'l Bank of Boston	Williams Trust Co.	Phila. Trust Co.	Elm Street Trust Co.	Total
Retail lock-box	1 415	-	962	-	2 377
Wholesale lock-box	-	3 250	-	-	3 250
Over-the-counter	480	-	-	-	480
Total	1 895	3 250	962	-	6 107

Disbursements					
General disbursements	1 325	2 020	565	1	3 911
Payroll	-	-	-	-	-
Total	1 325	2 020	565	1	3 911

| Net transfers to (from) Headquarters | 570 | 1 230 | 397 | (1) | 2 196 |

CASH ALPHA – BANK ACCOUNT SUMMARY

BANK 3rd National Bank of Boston	DATE ACCT. OPENED 1885	ADMINISTERED BY Boston Acctg. Cente
STREET ADDRESS 4047 Milk Street	CITY, STATE & ZIP CODE Boston, Mass. 02106	BANK TEL. NO.

OFFICERS & CONTACTS		BANK SIZE			
L. Frederick Pringle	Chairman			AMOUNT (M Dollars)	STATUS
Bertram P. Samuels	President				1966	19
George R. Jones	Sr. VP	TOTAL DEPOSITS		619	
William D. Morrison	VP	LOCAL CAPITAL		62	
Robert T. McLeod	VP	LOAN LIMIT		5.9	
Edw. R. Donohue	VP	RANK BY SIZE	U.S.		71	7
			STATE		4	
			CITY		3	
		NO. OF BRANCHES		19	

BANKING ACTIVITY (MONTHLY)

COMPANY UNIT	ACCOUNT TITLE	BALANCES (K$)		VOLUMES (K$)		NO. OF CHECKS		TRANSFERS (TO (FROM)
		CO. LEDGER	BANK–NCB	DEPOSITS	PAYMENTS	DEPOSIT	PAYMENT	
Boston A/C	Regular	946	1,125	480	1,325	1,540	4,180	ESTCo NH
	Retail L/B	–	–	1,415	–	33,600	–	MN NYC
	Total	946	1,125	1,895	1,325	35,140	4,180	

MONTHLY ACCOUNT ANALYSIS

SERVICE CHARGE CREDITS LESS ACTIVITY CHARGES		COMPETITIVE BASIS	BANK BASIS	INCREMENTAL BAS
AVG. DAILY BALANCES	COMPANY LEDGER	$ 946,000	$ 946,000	
	PLUS: FLOAT GENERATED BY DISBURSING	241,000	241,000	
GROSS BANK STATEMENT BALANCES		$ 1,187,000	$1,187,000	
LESS: CHECKS IN TRANSIT		62,000	62,000	
NET COLLECTED BALANCE		$ 1,125,000	$1,125,000	
LESS: FEDERAL RESERVE: 16½ %		185,626	–	
AVAILABLE FOR INVESTMENT		$ 939,375	–	
EARNINGS	ON AFI: COMPETITIVE 5% %; BANK 2% %	$ 3,914.07	$ 1,875.00	
	ON TAXES: COMPETITIVE %; BANK %	–	–	
	TOTAL	$ 3,914.07	$ 1,875.00	
LESS ACTIVITY CHARGES (DETAILED BELOW)		1,592.50	1,408.20	
SERVICE CHARGE CREDITS LESS ACTIVITY CHARGES		$ 2,321.57	466.80	

ACTIVITY CHARGES		ITEMS	RATE	PRICE	RATE	PRICE
CHECKS PAID		4,180	.05	209.00	.05	209.00
CHECKS DEPOSITED	REGULAR	1,540	.02	30.80	.03	46.20
	RETAIL LOCK BOX	33,600	.0375	1,260.00	.03	1,008.00
	WHOLESALE LOCK BOX					
DEPOSIT TICKETS						
INTERBRANCH DEPOSITS						
TRANSFERS		30	1.00	30.00	1.50	45.00
RETURNED CHECKS						
STOP PAYMENTS						
ACCOUNT RECONCILIATION		4,180	.015	62.70	Flat	100.00
TOTAL ACTIVITY CHARGES				1,592.50		1,408.20

| O. UNIT NEFITING | IDENTIFICATION | RATE | DATED | MATURITY | AMOUNT OF LOAN | | |
					ORIGINAL	BALANCE	AS OF
None	(Bank participated in major term loans in the forties)						

REEMENT ON COMPENSATING BALANCE   No agreement.

LICY CONSTRAINTS   Confidential: NCB should be at least $500,000, as a "call" on $5,000,000. Internal constraint: tax payments should provide no more than 1/3 of the total earnings credit.

| VALUE OF INTANGIBLE SERVICES | | | |
	PER MONTH	PER YEAR	COMMENT
NERAL ADVISORY			
TERNATIONAL			
W BUSINESS			
RGERS & ACQUISITIONS			
EDIT INFORMATION			
TOTAL			

MARKS: This is Ancama's oldest banking relationship. In the late forties, before the closing of the Boston plant, net collected balances exceeded $2.5 million. The bank still measures the present relationship against the past, rather than in terms of current profitability.

The bank admits that the 2.0% service charge credit on NCB is out-of-date, but it claims that its activity cost figures are far below the bank's actual costs, and that, overall, its cost structure is competitive with other Boston banks.

Surprisingly, the bank has agreed to accept tax payments in lieu of a portion (unspecified) of balances. Tax payments are to earn a credit equal to interest of 1.65% for 20 days. Internal constraint: tax payments should provide no more than 1/3 of the total earnings credit.

ONG RANGE PLANS   Despite our long history with this bank, its cost structure makes it a candidate for major review in April '68.

95

CASH ALPHA – BANK ACCOUNT SUMMARY

BANK	DATE ACCT. OPENED	ADMINISTERED BY
Williams Trust Company	1909	Boston Acctg. Center

STREET ADDRESS	CITY, STATE & ZIP CODE	BANK TEL. NO.
7306 Water Street	Boston, Mass. 02106	

OFFICERS & CONTACTS / BANK SIZE

OFFICERS & CONTACTS		BANK SIZE		
Peter A. Scheides	Chairman		AMOUNT (M Dollars)	STATUS
Matthew M. Moore	President			19 66 19
Alfred D. Little	Exec. VP	TOTAL DEPOSITS	485	
Paul F. Forest	VP	LOCAL CAPITAL	52	
John C. Schwartz	VP	LOAN LIMIT	5	
William R. Grey	AVP	RANK BY SIZE — U.S.		183 17
		STATE		5
		CITY		4
		NO. OF BRANCHES		12 1

BANKING ACTIVITY (MONTHLY)

COMPANY UNIT	ACCOUNT TITLE	BALANCES (K$)		VOLUMES (K$)		NO. OF CHECKS		TRANSFERS (K$) TO (FROM)
		CO. LEDGER	BANK–NCB	DEPOSITS	PAYMENTS	DEPOSIT	PAYMENT	
Boston A/C	Regular	150	209	–	–	–	–	MN – NYC
	Wholesale L/B	–	–	3,250	–	4,420	–	
	Payroll	–	*	–	2,020	–	3,460	
	Total	150	209	3,250	2,020	4,420	3,460	

* Automatic daily transfer from regular account to payroll account to pay incoming checks.

MONTHLY ACCOUNT ANALYSIS

SERVICE CHARGE CREDITS LESS ACTIVITY CHARGES		COMPETITIVE BASIS	BANK BASIS	INCREMENTAL BASIS
AVG. DAILY BALANCES	COMPANY LEDGER	$ 150,000	$ 150,000	
	PLUS: FLOAT GENERATED BY DISBURSING	243,000	243,000	
GROSS BANK STATEMENT BALANCES		$ 393,000	$ 393,000	
LESS: CHECKS IN TRANSIT		184,000	184,000	
NET COLLECTED BALANCE		$ 209,000	$ 209,000	
LESS: FEDERAL RESERVE: 16½ %		34,485	34,485	
AVAILABLE FOR INVESTMENT		$ 174,515	$ 174,515	
EARNINGS	ON AFT COMPETITIVE 5 %; BANK 3.75 %	$ 727.15	$ 545.36	
	ON TAXES: COMPETITIVE %; BANK %	–	–	
	TOTAL	$ 727.15	$ 545.36	727.20
LESS ACTIVITY CHARGES (DETAILED BELOW)		537.20	539.41	400.00
SERVICE CHARGE CREDITS LESS ACTIVITY CHARGES		$ 189.95	$ 5.95	$ 327.20

ACTIVITY CHARGES		ITEMS	RATE	PRICE	RATE	PRICE	
CHECKS PAID		3,460	.05	173.00	.05	173.00	
CHECKS DEPOSITED	REGULAR						
	RETAIL LOCK BOX						
	WHOLESALE LOCK BOX	4,420	.065	287.30	.068	300.56	.8 @ 500 400
DEPOSIT TICKETS							
INTERBRANCH DEPOSITS							
TRANSFERS		25	1.00	25.00	1.25	31.25	
RETURNED CHECKS							
STOP PAYMENTS							
ACCOUNT RECONCILIATION		3,460	.015	51.90	.01	34.60	
TOTAL ACTIVITY CHARGES				$537.20		$539.41	$ 400.

LOAN ACTIVITY

CO. UNIT BENEFITING	IDENTIFICATION	RATE	DATED	MATURITY	AMOUNT OF LOAN		
					ORIGINAL	BALANCE	AS OF
	None						

AGREEMENT ON COMPENSATING BALANCE

POLICY CONSTRAINTS

VALUE OF INTANGIBLE SERVICES			
	PER MONTH	PER YEAR	COMMENT
GENERAL ADVISORY	$ 150	$ 1,800	
INTERNATIONAL			
NEW BUSINESS			
MERGERS & ACQUISITIONS			
CREDIT INFORMATION			
TOTAL	$ 150	$ 1,800	

REMARKS: Discussions in January '67:

(1) Did not review all charges, as the present rates had been negotiated in early '66.
(2) Bank agreed to service charge credit on tax payments ...15 days at 3.75%.
(3) Credit for tax payments not to exceed 1/2 of total service charge credit.

LONG RANGE PLANS

No major change.

BANK		DATE ACCT. OPENED	ADMINISTERED BY
Philadelphia Trust Company		1944	Boston Acctg. Center

STREET ADDRESS	CITY, STATE & ZIP CODE	BANK TEL. NO.
1776 Chestnut Street	Philadelphia, Pa. 19101	

OFFICERS & CONTACTS		BANK SIZE			
			AMOUNT (M Dollars)	STATUS 19 66	1965
Benjamin F. Smyth	Chairman				
George R. Paine	President				
Thomas D. Franklin	Sr. VP	TOTAL DEPOSITS	1307		
J.T. Hamilton	VP	LOCAL CAPITAL	129		
William L. Lee	VP	LOAN LIMIT	11		
		RANK BY SIZE — U.S.		29	31
		STATE		3	3
		CITY		2	2
		NO. OF BRANCHES		19	16

BANKING ACTIVITY (MONTHLY)

COMPANY UNIT	ACCOUNT TITLE	BALANCES (K$)		VOLUMES (K$)		NO. OF CHECKS		TRANSFERS (K$) TO (FROM)
		CO. LEDGER	BANK–NCB	DEPOSITS	PAYMENTS	DEPOSIT	PAYMENT	
Boston A/C	Regular	271	325	-	565	-	940	MN – NYC
	Retail L/B	-	-	962	-	23,800		
	Total	271	325	962	565	23,800	940	

MONTHLY ACCOUNT ANALYSIS

SERVICE CHARGE CREDITS LESS ACTIVITY CHARGES		COMPETITIVE BASIS	BANK BASIS	INCREMENTAL BASIS
AVG. DAILY BALANCES	COMPANY LEDGER	$ 271,000	$ 271,000	
	PLUS: FLOAT GENERATED BY DISBURSING	107,000	107,000	
GROSS BANK STATEMENT BALANCES		$ 378,000	$ 378,000	
LESS: CHECKS IN TRANSIT		53,000	53,000	
NET COLLECTED BALANCE		$ 325,000	$ 325,000	
LESS: FEDERAL RESERVE: $16\frac{1}{2}$ %		53,625	-	
AVAILABLE FOR INVESTMENT		$ 271,375	-	
EARNINGS	ON AFT COMPETITIVE 5 %; BANK 3.5 %	$ 1,130.73	$ 947.92	
	ON TAXES: COMPETITIVE % ; BANK %	-	-	
	TOTAL	$ 1,130.73	$ 947.92	
LESS ACTIVITY CHARGES (DETAILED BELOW)		983.60	919.40	
SERVICE CHARGE CREDITS LESS ACTIVITY CHARGES		$ 147.13	$ 28.52	

ACTIVITY CHARGES		ITEMS	RATE	PRICE	RATE	PRICE	
CHECKS PAID							
CHECKS DEPOSITED	REGULAR	940	.05	47.00	.05	47.00	
	RETAIL LOCK BOX	23,800	.0375	892.50	.035	833.00	
	WHOLESALE LOCK BOX						
DEPOSIT TICKETS							
INTERBRANCH DEPOSITS							
TRANSFERS		30	1.00	30.00	1.00	30.00	
RETURNED CHECKS							
STOP PAYMENTS							
ACCOUNT RECONCILIATION		940	.015	14.10	.01	9.40	
TOTAL ACTIVITY CHARGES				$983.60		$919.40	

LOAN ACTIVITY

CO. UNIT BENEFITING	IDENTIFICATION	RATE	DATED	MATURITY	AMOUNT OF LOAN		AS OF
					ORIGINAL	BALANCE	
None							

AGREEMENT ON COMPENSATING BALANCE

POLICY CONSTRAINTS

VALUE OF INTANGIBLE SERVICES			
	PER MONTH	PER YEAR	COMMENT
GENERAL ADVISORY			
INTERNATIONAL			
NEW BUSINESS			
MERGERS & ACQUISITIONS			
CREDIT INFORMATION			
TOTAL			

REMARKS:

Agreement reach January '67:

(1) Service charge credit on tax payments ... 20 days at 3.15%, no limits.
(2) Agreeable to a cash fee for service charge shortfall, at 125% of analysis shortage, cumulative, payable every six months. Bank would not like to see us use this route exclusively, but has no objection to compensation that is 2/3 fee, 1/3 balances, tax payments, etc.

LONG RANGE PLANS

No changes foreseen, except in terms of compensation.

BANK	DATE ACCT. OPENED	ADMINISTERED BY
Elm Street Trust Company	1923	Boston Acctg. Center
STREET ADDRESS	CITY, STATE & ZIP CODE	BANK TEL. NO.
982 Chapel Street	New Haven, Connecticut	

OFFICERS & CONTACTS		BANK SIZE		STATUS	
			AMOUNT (M Dollars)	1966	1965
Earl J. Miller	Chairman				
Gordon S. Cochrane	President				
Eugene N. Babb	Sr. VP	TOTAL DEPOSITS	673		
William A. Davis	VP	LOCAL CAPITAL	67		
Robert F. Eli	AVP	LOAN LIMIT	6		
		RANK BY SIZE	U.S.	61	64
			STATE	3	3
			CITY	1	1
		NO. OF BRANCHES			

BANKING ACTIVITY (MONTHLY)

COMPANY UNIT	ACCOUNT TITLE	BALANCES (K$)		VOLUMES (K$)		NO. OF CHECKS		TRANSFERS (K$) TO (FROM)
		CO. LEDGER	BANK–NCB	DEPOSITS	PAYMENTS	DEPOSIT	PAYMENT	
Boston A/C	Regular	125	125	–	1	–	20	(MNB–NY)
	Emergency	25	25					
	Total	150	150	–	1	–	20	

MONTHLY ACCOUNT ANALYSIS

SERVICE CHARGE CREDITS LESS ACTIVITY CHARGES		COMPETITIVE BASIS	BANK BASIS	INCREMENTAL BASIS
AVG. DAILY BALANCES	COMPANY LEDGER	$ 150,000	Not requested	
	PLUS: FLOAT GENERATED BY DISBURSING	–		
GROSS BANK STATEMENT BALANCES		$ 150,000		
LESS: CHECKS IN TRANSIT		–		
NET COLLECTED BALANCE		$ 150,000		
LESS: FEDERAL RESERVE: $16\frac{1}{2}$ %		24,750		
AVAILABLE FOR INVESTMENT		$ 125,250		
EARNINGS	ON AFI: COMPETITIVE 5 %; BANK %	$ 521.88		
	ON TAXES: COMPETITIVE %; BANK %	–		
	TOTAL	$ 521.88		
LESS ACTIVITY CHARGES (DETAILED BELOW)		1.00		
SERVICE CHARGE CREDITS LESS ACTIVITY CHARGES		$ 520.88		

ACTIVITY CHARGES		ITEMS	RATE	PRICE	RATE	PRICE
CHECKS PAID		20	.05	1.00		
CHECKS DEPOSITED	REGULAR					
	RETAIL LOCK BOX					
	WHOLESALE LOCK BOX					
DEPOSIT TICKETS						
INTERBRANCH DEPOSITS						
TRANSFERS						
RETURNED CHECKS						
STOP PAYMENTS						
ACCOUNT RECONCILIATION						
TOTAL ACTIVITY CHARGES				1.00		

LOAN ACTIVITY

CO. UNIT BENEFITING	IDENTIFICATION	RATE	DATED	MATURITY	AMOUNT OF LOAN		
					ORIGINAL	BALANCE	AS OF
	None						

AGREEMENT ON COMPENSATING BALANCE

POLICY CONSTRAINTS   See Remarks:

VALUE OF INTANGIBLE SERVICES			
	PER MONTH	PER YEAR	COMMENT
GENERAL ADVISORY			
INTERNATIONAL			
NEW BUSINESS			
MERGERS & ACQUISITIONS			
CREDIT INFORMATION			
TOTAL			

REMARKS: When disbursing was moved out of the New Haven plant and into the Boston Accounting Center, it was decided to maintain a good bank balance with Elm Street Trust, even though significant services were no longer required.

In this case, as in the case of the 3rd National Bank of South Bend, it is difficult to quantify the annual value of this relationship. At the present time, it seems that we have no better basis to measure what this relationship should be than our feelings in '63 that $150,000 was about right.

LONG RANGE PLANS
No change.

San Francisco Accounting Center
Monthly   - $K

	U.S.Nat'l. Bank of Calif.	Union Trust Co.	Los Angeles Trust Co.	Sunnyville Trust Co.	Total
Receipts					
Retail lock-box	2 470	--	--	--	2 470
Wholesale lock-box	2 150	3 440	--	--	5 590
Over-the-counter	200	--	--	--	200
Total	4 820	3 440	--	--	8 260
Disbursements					
Gen'l disbursements	2 875	1 435	1 500	4	5 814
Payroll	1 200	--	--	--	1 200
Total	4 075	1 435	1 500	4	7 014
Net transfers to headquarters	745	2 005	(1 500)	(4)	1 246

CASH ALPHA - BANK ACCOUNT SUMMARY

BANK		DATE ACCT. OPENED	ADMINISTERED BY
U.S. National Bank of California			S.F. Acctg. Center
STREET ADDRESS	CITY, STATE & ZIP CODE		BANK TEL. NO.
411 Water Street	San Francisco, California		

OFFICERS & CONTACTS		BANK SIZE			
Harold L. Norris	Chairman of the Board		AMOUNT (M Dollars)	STATUS	
Peter J. Sieppe	President			19 66	19 65
Marcus R. Heise	Sr. VP	TOTAL DEPOSITS	4,111		
John J. McTeague	Sr. VP	LOCAL CAPITAL	402		
Anthony L. Peters	VP	' OAN LIMIT	35		
		RANK BY SIZE — U.S.		10	11
		STATE		2	2
		CITY		2	2
		NO. OF BRANCHES		207	191

BANKING ACTIVITY (MONTHLY)

COMPANY UNIT	ACCOUNT TITLE	BALANCES (K$)		VOLUMES (K$)		NO. OF CHECKS		TRANSFERS (K$) TO (FROM)
		CO. LEDGER	BANK—NCB	DEPOSITS	PAYMENTS	DEPOSIT	PAYMENT	
S.F. A/C	Regular	0	616	200	2,875	650	2,350	WSTCo—NYC
	Payroll	-	0 *	-	1,200	-	1,950	
	Retail L/B	-	-	2,470	-	55,100	-	
	Wholesale L/B	-	-	2,150	-	3,060	-	
	Total	0	616	4,820	4,075	58,810	4,300	

*Automatic daily transfer from payroll account to regular account to pay incoming checks.

MONTHLY ACCOUNT ANALYSIS

SERVICE CHARGE CREDITS LESS ACTIVITY CHARGES		COMPETITIVE BASIS	BANK BASIS	INCREMENTAL BASIS
AVG. DAILY BALANCES	COMPANY LEDGER	0	0	
	PLUS: FLOAT GENERATED BY DISBURSING	$ 841,000	$ 841,000	
GROSS BANK STATEMENT BALANCES		$ 841,000	$ 841,000	
LESS: CHECKS IN TRANSIT		225,000	225,000	
NET COLLECTED BALANCE		$ 616,000	$ 616,000	
LESS: FEDERAL RESERVE: 16½ %		51,436	51,436	
AVAILABLE FOR INVESTMENT		$ 564,564	$ 564,564	
EARNINGS	ON AFI: COMPETITIVE 5 %; BANK 3.875 %	$ 2,352.35	$ 1,823.07	
	ON TAXES: COMPETITIVE %; BANK 3 %	1,268.75	652.34	
	TOTAL $625K/mo. for 15 days	$ 3,621.10	$ 2,475.41	$3,621.10
LESS ACTIVITY CHARGES (DETAILED BELOW) after 16½% res.		2,548.40	2,336.12	1,900.00
SERVICE CHARGE CREDITS LESS ACTIVITY CHARGES		$ 1,072.70	$ 139.29	$1,721.10

ACTIVITY CHARGES		ITEMS	RATE	PRICE	RATE	PRICE		
CHECKS PAID		4,300	.05	215.00	.05	215.00		
CHECKS DEPOSITED	REGULAR	650	.02	13.00	.02	13.00		
	RETAIL LOCK BOX	55,100	.0375	2,066.25	.034	1,873.40	2 @ 500	1000
	WHOLESALE LOCK BOX	3,060	.065	198.90	.062	189.72	1 @ 500	500
DEPOSIT TICKETS							1/2 @ 800	400
INTERBRANCH DEPOSITS								
TRANSFERS		20	1.00	20.00	1.00	20.00		
RETURNED CHECKS								
STOP PAYMENTS								
ACCOUNT RECONCILIATION		2,350	.015	35.25	flat	25.00		
TOTAL ACTIVITY CHARGES				2,548.40		2,336.12		1900.00

103

LOAN ACTIVITY

CO. UNIT BENEFITING	IDENTIFICATION	RATE	DATED	MATURITY	AMOUNT OF LOAN		AS C
					ORIGINAL	BALANCE	
	None.						

AGREEMENT ON COMPENSATING BALANCE

POLICY CONSTRAINTS   Internal guideline: NCB at least $500,000

VALUE OF INTANGIBLE SERVICES			
	PER MONTH	PER YEAR	COMMENT
GENERAL ADVISORY			
INTERNATIONAL			
NEW BUSINESS			
MERGERS & ACQUISITIONS			
CREDIT INFORMATION	$ 333	$ 4,000	
TOTAL	$ 333	$ 4,000	

REMARKS:

Agreement reached January '67:

(1) Schedule of service charges and credit on balances unchanged.
(2) Service charge credit on tax payments ... still 15 days at 3%.
(3) Credit for tax payments not to exceed 1/3 of total service charge credit.
(4) Agrees to cash fee for service charge shortfall, at 130% of analysis basis.

(Internal policy guideline: NCB at least $500,000).

LONG RANGE PLANS

No change.

ANK	DATE ACCT. OPENED	ADMINISTERED BY
Union Trust Company of Los Angeles	1954	S.F. Acctg. Center

REET ADDRESS	CITY, STATE & ZIP CODE	BANK TEL. NO.
25 Wilshire Boulevard	Los Angeles, California 90054	

BANK SIZE

OFFICERS & CONTACTS			AMOUNT (M Dollars)	STATUS 1966	1965
avid A. Lewis	Chairman				
ohn R. Mathews	President				
eorge T. Grant	Sr. VP	TOTAL DEPOSITS	1,153		
arold M. Harris	VP	LOCAL CAPITAL	96		
acob O. Watson	VP	LOAN LIMIT	9		
homas A. Jones	VP	RANK BY SIZE — U.S.		31	4
		STATE		7	7
		CITY		4	4
		NO. OF BRANCHES		39	35

BANKING ACTIVITY (MONTHLY)

COMPANY UNIT	ACCOUNT TITLE	BALANCES (K$) CO. LEDGER	BANK–NCB	VOLUMES (K$) DEPOSITS	PAYMENTS	NO. OF CHECKS DEPOSIT	PAYMENT	TRANSFERS (K$) TO (FROM)
.F. A/C	Regular	184	350	–	1,435	–	1,175	LATCO-LA
	Wholesale L/B	–	–	3,440	–	4,870	–	WST-NYC
Total		184	350	3,440	1,435	4,870	1,175	

MONTHLY ACCOUNT ANALYSIS

SERVICE CHARGE CREDITS LESS ACTIVITY CHARGES		COMPETITIVE BASIS	BANK BASIS	INCREMENTAL BASIS
AVG. DAILY BALANCES	COMPANY LEDGER	$ 184,000	$ 184,000	
	PLUS: FLOAT GENERATED BY DISBURSING	350,000	350,000	
GROSS BANK STATEMENT BALANCES		$ 534,000	$ 534,000	
LESS: CHECKS IN TRANSIT		184,000	184,000	
NET COLLECTED BALANCE		$ 350,000	$ 350,000	
LESS: FEDERAL RESERVE: %		57,750	57,750	
AVAILABLE FOR INVESTMENT		$ 292,250	$ 292,250	
EARNINGS	ON AFI COMPETITIVE 5 %; BANK 3-1/4 %	$ 1,217.71	$ 791.51	
	ON TAXES: COMPETITIVE %; BANK %	–	–	
	TOTAL	$ 1,217.71	$ 791.51	$ 1,217.71
LESS ACTIVITY CHARGES (DETAILED BELOW)		427.93	416.18	480.00
SERVICE CHARGE CREDITS LESS ACTIVITY CHARGES		$ 789.78	$ 375.33	$ 737.71

ACTIVITY CHARGES	ITEMS	RATE	PRICE	RATE	PRICE		
CHECKS PAID	1,175	.05	58.75	.04	47.00		
CHECKS DEPOSITED — REGULAR							
RETAIL LOCK BOX							
WHOLESALE LOCK BOX	4,870	.065	316.55	.065	316.55	.8 @ 400	320
DEPOSIT TICKETS						.2 @ 800	160
INTERBRANCH DEPOSITS							
TRANSFERS	35		35.00	1.00	35.00		
RETURNED CHECKS							
STOP PAYMENTS							
ACCOUNT RECONCILIATION	1,175	.015	17.63	.015	17.63		
TOTAL ACTIVITY CHARGES			427.93		416.18		480

LOAN ACTIVITY

CO. UNIT BENEFITING	IDENTIFICATION	RATE	DATED	MATURITY	AMOUNT OF LOAN		AS OF
					ORIGINAL	BALANCE	

AGREEMENT ON COMPENSATING BALANCE

POLICY CONSTRAINTS   Internal policy guideline: maintain NCB at the $350,000 level.

VALUE OF INTANGIBLE SERVICES			
	PER MONTH	PER YEAR	COMMENT
GENERAL ADVISORY			
INTERNATIONAL			
NEW BUSINESS	$ 833	$ 10,000	Industrial Roundtable Program
MERGERS & ACQUISITIONS			
CREDIT INFORMATION			
Real Estate	833	10,000	Retail Store Expansion Program
TOTAL	$1,666	$ 20,000	

REMARKS: The value of tangibles and intangibles taken together exceeds the value of the balances to the bank. Because of the intangibles, we should not disturb this relationship.

LONG RANGE PLANS   Review for possibility of liberalizing balances in April '68.

106

BANK		DATE ACCT. OPENED	ADMINISTERED BY
Los Angeles Trust Company		1954	S.F. Acctg. Center
STREET ADDRESS	CITY, STATE & ZIP CODE		BANK TEL. NO.
24 Wilshire Blvd.	Los Angeles, California 90054		

OFFICERS & CONTACTS

		BANK SIZE		
Horace L. MacKenzie	Chairman		AMOUNT (M Dollars)	STATUS 1966 / 1965
Herman T. Sharp	President			
Charles V. Williams	Sr. VP	TOTAL DEPOSITS	2,012	
Alexander I. Matthews	VP	LOCAL CAPITAL	190	
Theodore B. Kelly	VP	LOAN LIMIT	18	
		RANK BY SIZE — U.S.		19 / 20
		STATE		5 / 5
		CITY		2 / 2
		NO. OF BRANCHES		91 / 87

BANKING ACTIVITY (MONTHLY)

COMPANY UNIT	ACCOUNT TITLE	BALANCES (K$) CO. LEDGER	BALANCES (K$) BANK–NCB	VOLUMES (K$) DEPOSITS	VOLUMES (K$) PAYMENTS	NO. OF CHECKS DEPOSIT	NO. OF CHECKS PAYMENT	TRANSFERS (K$) TO (FROM)
S.F. A/C	Regular	-0-	267	–	1,500	–	1,914	(Union Trst)
	Total	-0-	267	–	1,500	–	1,914	

MONTHLY ACCOUNT ANALYSIS

SERVICE CHARGE CREDITS LESS ACTIVITY CHARGES		COMPETITIVE BASIS	BANK BASIS	INCREMENTAL BASIS
AVG. DAILY BALANCES	COMPANY LEDGER	-0-	Not requested	
	PLUS: FLOAT GENERATED BY DISBURSING	267,000		
GROSS BANK STATEMENT BALANCES		$ 267,000		
LESS: CHECKS IN TRANSIT		–		
NET COLLECTED BALANCE		$ 267,000		
LESS: FEDERAL RESERVE: 16½%		44,055		
AVAILABLE FOR INVESTMENT		$ 222,945		
EARNINGS	ON AFI COMPETITIVE 5 %; BANK %	928.94		
	ON TAXES: COMPETITIVE %; BANK %	–		
	TOTAL	$ 928.94		
LESS ACTIVITY CHARGES (DETAILED BELOW)		95.70		
SERVICE CHARGE CREDITS LESS ACTIVITY CHARGES		$ 833.24		

ACTIVITY CHARGES		ITEMS	RATE	PRICE	RATE	PRICE	
CHECKS PAID		1,914	.05	95.70			
CHECKS DEPOSITED	REGULAR						
	RETAIL LOCK BOX						
	WHOLESALE LOCK BOX						
DEPOSIT TICKETS							
INTERBRANCH DEPOSITS							
TRANSFERS							
RETURNED CHECKS							
STOP PAYMENTS							
ACCOUNT RECONCILIATION							
TOTAL ACTIVITY CHARGES				95.70			

LOAN ACTIVITY

CO. UNIT BENEFITING	IDENTIFICATION	RATE	DATED	MATURITY	AMOUNT OF LOAN		
					ORIGINAL	BALANCE	AS OF
None							

AGREEMENT ON COMPENSATING BALANCE

POLICY CONSTRAINTS

VALUE OF INTANGIBLE SERVICES			
	PER MONTH	PER YEAR	COMMENT
GENERAL ADVISORY			
INTERNATIONAL			
NEW BUSINESS			
MERGERS & ACQUISITIONS			
CREDIT INFORMATION			
TOTAL	**-0-**	**-0-**	

REMARKS: Jack Scott of the Flower Street office of this bank was of particular help to Ancama when we opened the L.A. Division office in 1954, introducing our sales people throughout the business community, developing credit and general business condition information, and being of general service to the Division. When he left the bank, no one took his place in terms of the intangible services he had been providing. In consequence, the Division has developed far closer ties with the Union Trust Company. This account is no longer needed.

LONG RANGE PLANS   Close this account.

108

CASH ALPHA – BANK ACCOUNT SUMMARY

BANK Sunnyville Trust Company	DATE ACCT. OPENED 1957	ADMINISTERED BY S.F. Acctg. Center
STREET ADDRESS 888 Main Street	CITY, STATE & ZIP CODE Sunnyville, California	BANK TEL. NO.

OFFICERS & CONTACTS		BANK SIZE		
Jack Mason	Chairman		AMOUNT (M Dollars)	STATUS 19 66 / 19 65
Leonard L. Wilson	President			
Max M. Sampson	Sr. VP	TOTAL DEPOSITS	121	
Geo. R. Richards	VP	LOCAL CAPITAL	10	
Harold T. Love	VP	LOAN LIMIT	1.0	
		RANK BY SIZE — U.S.		316 / 319
		STATE		19 / 18
		CITY		1 / 1
		NO. OF BRANCHES		2 / 2

BANKING ACTIVITY (MONTHLY)

COMPANY UNIT	ACCOUNT TITLE	BALANCES (K$)		VOLUMES (K$)		NO. OF CHECKS		TRANSFERS (K$) TO (FROM)
		CO. LEDGER	BANK–NCB	DEPOSITS	PAYMENTS	DEPOSIT	PAYMENT	
S.F. A/C	Regular	75	75	–	–	–	–	(USNB – SF)
	Emergency	25	24	–	4	–	17	
		100	99	–	4	–	17	

MONTHLY ACCOUNT ANALYSIS

SERVICE CHARGE CREDITS LESS ACTIVITY CHARGES		COMPETITIVE BASIS	BANK BASIS	INCREMENTAL BASIS
AVG. DAILY BALANCES	COMPANY LEDGER	$ 100,000		
	PLUS: FLOAT GENERATED BY DISBURSING	–		
GROSS BANK STATEMENT BALANCES		$ 100,000		
LESS: CHECKS IN TRANSIT		1,000		
NET COLLECTED BALANCE		$ 99,000		
LESS: FEDERAL RESERVE: $16\frac{1}{2}$ %		16,335		
AVAILABLE FOR INVESTMENT		$ 82,665		
EARNINGS	ON AFI COMPETITIVE 5 %; BANK %	$ 344.44		
	ON TAXES: COMPETITIVE %; BANK %	–		
	TOTAL	$ 344.44		
LESS ACTIVITY CHARGES (DETAILED BELOW)		.85		
SERVICE CHARGE CREDITS LESS ACTIVITY CHARGES		$ 343.59		

ACTIVITY CHARGES		ITEMS	RATE	PRICE	RATE	PRICE	
CHECKS PAID		17	.05	.85			
CHECKS DEPOSITED	REGULAR						
	RETAIL LOCK BOX						
	WHOLESALE LOCK BOX	✓					
DEPOSIT TICKETS							
INTERBRANCH DEPOSITS							
TRANSFERS							
RETURNED CHECKS							
STOP PAYMENTS							
ACCOUNT RECONCILIATION							
TOTAL ACTIVITY CHARGES				.85			

LOAN ACTIVITY

CO. UNIT BENEFITING	IDENTIFICATION	RATE	DATED	MATURITY	AMOUNT OF LOAN		AS OF
					ORIGINAL	BALANCE	

AGREEMENT ON COMPENSATING BALANCE

POLICY CONSTRAINTS

VALUE OF INTANGIBLE SERVICES			
	PER MONTH	PER YEAR	COMMENT
GENERAL ADVISORY			
INTERNATIONAL			
NEW BUSINESS			
MERGERS & ACQUISITIONS			
CREDIT INFORMATION			
TOTAL			

REMARKS:

When disbursing was moved out of the Sunnyville plant and into the San Francisco Accounting Center, it was decided to maintain a good bank relationship with the Sunnyville Trust, even though significant services were no longer required.

In this case, as in the case of the 3rd National Bank of South Bend, it is difficult to quantify the annual value of this relationship. At this time, it seems that we have no better basis for measuring what this relationship should be than our feelings in '63 that $100,000 was about right.

LONG RANGE PLANS

No change for the time being.

Ancama Corporation
Schematic Diagram of Banking Relations

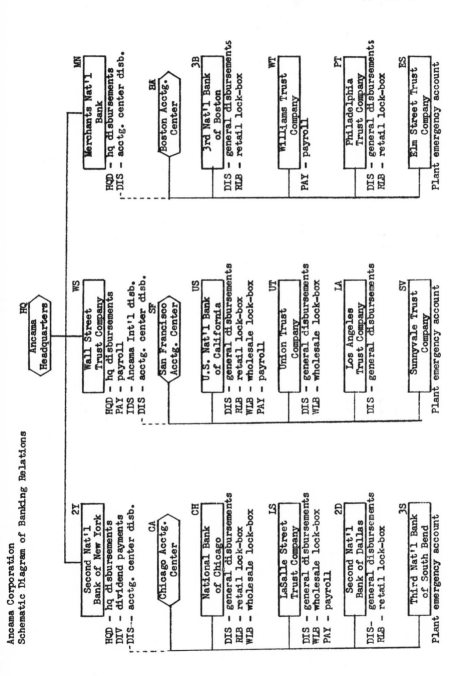

Ancama Corporation - Summary of CASH ALPHA Test Results

	(1) Base Case	(2) Alternate 1- Increased use of taxes	(3) Alternate 1- vs. Base Case	(4) Alternate 2- Reduced call on credit	(5) Alternate 2- vs. Alternate 1	(6) Alternate 3- CH charge sched. at 2D	(7) Alternate 3- vs. Alternate 2	(8) Alternate 4- Test of GF lock-box	(9) Alternate 4- vs. Alternate 3	(10) Alternate 4- vs. Base Case
1- TOBAL	$6,936,354.69	$6,586,354.69	- 350,000.00	$5,582,906.13	-1,003,448.56	$4,974,872.61	- 608,033.52	$4,717,030.98	- 257,841.63	-2,219,323.71
2- TORCV	494,054.00	494,054.00	-	494,054.00	-	494,054.00		525,470.19	31,416.19	31,416.19
3- TOBAL + TORCV	$7,430,408.69	$7,080,408.69	- 350,000.00	$6,076,960.13	-1,003,448.56	$5,468,926.61	- 608,033.52	$5,242,501.17	- 226,425.44	-2,187,907.52
4-										
5- TOBAL @ 20% capital cost	$ 115,608.22	$ 109,774.77	- 5,833.45	$ 93,050.30	16,724.47	$ 82,916.20	10,134.10	78,618.76	4,297.44	36,989.46
6- TOFEE	326.85	326.85	-	347.49	20.64	970.28	622.79	1,124.93	154.65	798.08
7- Subtotal	$ 115,935.07	$ 110,101.62	- 5,833.45	$ 93,397.79	16,703.83	$ 83,886.48	9,511.31	79,743.69	4,142.79	36,191.38
8- Less artificial HQTAX credit	15.78	8.78	7.00	8.37	.41	5.42	2.95	.37	5.05	15.41
9- Solution cost-cash only	$ 115,919.29	$ 110,092.84	- 5,826.45	$ 93,389.42	16,703.42	$ 83,881.06	9,508.36	79,743.32	4,137.74	36,175.97
10- TORCV @ 20% capital cost	8,234.40	8,234.40	-	8,234.40	-	8,234.40		8,758.01	523.61	523.61
11- Total solution cost	$ 124,153.69	$ 118,327.24	- 5,826.45	$ 101,623.82	16,703.42	$ 92,115.46	9,508.36	88,501.33	3,614.13	35,652.36
12-										
13- TOBAL @ 6% capital cost	$ 34,681.77	$ 32,931.77	- 1,750.00	$ 27,914.53	5,017.24	$ 24,874.36	3,040.17	23,585.16	1,289.20	11,096.61
14- TOFEE	326.85	326.85	-	347.49	20.64	970.28	622.79	1,124.93	154.65	798.08
15- Subtotal	$ 35,008.62	$ 33,258.62	- 1,750.00	$ 28,262.02	4,996.60	$ 25,844.64	2,417.38	24,710.09	1,134.55	10,298.53
16- Less artificial HQTAX credit	15.78	8.78	7.00	8.37	.41	5.42	2.95	.37	5.05	15.41
17- Solution cost-cash only	$ 34,992.84	$ 33,249.84	- 1,743.00	$ 28,253.65	4,996.19	$ 25,839.22	2,414.43	24,709.72	1,129.50	10,283.12
18- TORCV @ 6% capital cost	2,470.27	2,470.27	-	2,470.27	-	2,470.27		2,627.35	157.08	157.08
19- Total solution cost	$ 37,463.11	$ 35,720.11	- 1,743.00	$ 30,723.92	4,996.19	$ 28,309.49	2,414.43	27,337.07	972.42	10,126.04
20-										
21- Cum. cost differential (line 11 basis)			5,826.45		22,529.87		32,038.23		35,652.36	35,652.36
22- Cum. cost differential (line 19 basis)			1,743.00		6,739.19		9,153.62		10,126.04	10,126.04
23-										
24- 2DFEE	-	-	-	-	-	-	-	-	-	-
25- CHFEE	$ 154.84	$ 154.84	-	$ 175.48	20.64	571.36	571.36	30.32	- 541.04	30.32
26- GFFEE	-	-	-	-	-	226.91	51.43	922.28	+ 695.37	767.44
27- PTFEE	-	-	-	-	-	-	-	-	-	-
28- USFEE	172.01	172.01	-	172.01	-	172.01	-	172.33	.32	.32
29- TOFEE	$ 326.85	$ 326.85	-	$ 347.49	20.64	970.28	622.79	1,124.93	154.65	798.08
30-										
31- 2DDIS	$4,299,647.79	$4,299,647.79	-	$4,299,647.79		$1,173,047.71	-3,126,600.08	37,638.88	-1,135,408.83	-4,262,008.91
32- 2YDIS	3,538,709.09	3,538,709.09	-	3,538,709.09		3,680,990.83	+142,281.74	3,903,791.73	+222,800.90	+365,082.64
33- CHDIS	564,084.74	564,084.74	-	1,761,643.12	+1,197,558.37	4,745,961.46	+2,984,318.34	5,138,645.67	+392,684.21	+4,574,560.93
34- ISDIS	1,197,558.37	1,197,558.37	-		-1,197,558.37					-1,197,558.37
35- GFDIS			-					519,923.72	519,923.72	519,923.72
36- CADIS	$9,600,000.00	$9,600,000.00	-	$9,600,000.00		$9,600,000.00		$9,600,000.00		
37-										
38- 3BDIS	$1,472,903.05	$1,472,903.05	-	$1,472,903.05		$1,472,903.05		656,909.20	- 815,993.85	- 815,993.85
39- MNDIS	417,096.95	417,096.95	-	417,096.95		417,096.95		1,233,090.80	+ 815,993.85	+ 815,993.85
40- PTDIS	-	-	-	-	-	-	-	-	-	-
41- BADIS	$1,890,000.00	$1,890,000.00	-	$1,890,000.00		$1,890,000.00		$1,890,000.00		

Ancama Corporation – Summary of CASH ALPHA Test Results

Line	(1) Base Case	(2) Alternate 1- Increased use of taxes	(3) Alternate 1- vs. Base Case	(4) Alternate 2- Reduced call on credit	(5) Alternate 2- vs. Alternate 1	(6) Alternate 3- CH charge sched. at 2D	(7) Alternate 3- vs. Alternate 2	(8) Alternate 4- Test of GF lock box	(9) Alternate 4- vs. Alternate 3	(10) Alternate 4- vs. Base Case
1- USDIS	$2,429,264.33	$2,429,264.33	--	$2,429,264.33	--	$2,429,264.33	--	$2,438,167.22	+ 8,902.89	+ 8,902.89
2- UTDIS			--		--		--		--	--
3- WSDIS	3,380,735.67	3,380,735.67	--	3,380,735.67	--	3,380,735.67	--	3,371,832.78	- 8,902.89	- 8,902.89
4- SFDIS	$5,810,000.00	$5,810,000.00	--	$5,810,000.00	--	$5,810,000.00	--	$5,810,000.00	--	--
5-										
6- 2YHQD	$10,255,000.00	$10,255,000.00	--	$10,255,000.00	--	$10,117,240.23	- 137,759.77	$9,901,520.36	-215,719.87	-353,479.64
7- MNHQD	1,465,000.00	1,465,000.00	--	1,465,000.00	--	1,602,759.77	+ 137,759.77	1,818,479.64	+215,719.87	+353,479.64
8- WSHQD	2,930,000.00	2,930,000.00	--	2,930,000.00	--	2,930,000.00	--	2,930,000.00	--	--
9- HQHQD										
10- NYHQD	$14,650,000.00	$14,650,000.00	--	$14,650,000.00	--	$14,650,000.00	--	$14,650,000.00	--	--
11-										
12- 2DTAX	$ 398,800.43	$ 398,800.43	--	$ 435,913.78	+ 37,113.35	$ 281,456.74	- 154,457.04	$ 14,938.07	-266,518.67	-383,862.36
13- 3PTAX		200,000.00	+ 200,000.00	200,000.00	--	435,913.78	+ 235,913.78	136,341.13	-299,572.65	+136,341.13
14- 3STAX	523,411.89	523,411.89	--	528,495.11	+ 5,083.22	200,000.00	- 328,495.11	200,000.00	--	-323,411.89
15- CHTAX		100,000.00	+ 100,000.00	100,000.00	--	541,162.53	+ 441,162.53	712,435.08	+171,272.55	+712,435.08
16- ESTAX			--		--	100,000.00	+ 100,000.00	100,000.00	--	+100,000.00
17- LSTAX										
18- PTTAX	584,836.32	584,836.32	--	584,836.32	--	584,836.32	--	1,484,808.08	+899,971.76	+899,971.76
19- SVTAX		100,000.00	+ 100,000.00	100,000.00	--	100,000.00	--	100,000.00	--	+100,000.00
20- USTAX	708,963.82	708,963.82	--	708,963.82	--	708,963.82	--	709,080.08	+ 116.26	+ 116.26
21- UTTAX		300,000.00	+ 300,000.00	300,000.00	--	300,000.00	--	300,000.00	--	+300,000.00
22- WTTAX	208,260.54	208,260.54	--	208,260.54	--	208,260.54	--	208,260.54	--	--
23- HQTAX	1,578,727.01	878,727.01	- 700,000.00	836,530.44	- 42,196.57	542,406.28	- 294,124.16	37,137.02	-505,269.26	-1,541,589.99
24- TOTAX	$4,003,000.00	$4,003,000.00	--	$4,003,000.00	--	$4,003,000.00	--	$4,003,000.00	--	--
25-										
26- 2DBAL	$ 562,301.91	$ 562,301.91	--	$ 541,886.24	- 20,415.64	$ 541,886.24	--	$ 174,300.49	-367,585.75	-388,001.42
27- 2YBAL	250,000.00	150,000.00	-100,000.00	150,000.00	--	150,000.00	--	150,000.00	--	-100,000.00
28- 3BBAL	813,751.39	813,751.39	--	580,718.51	- 233,032.88		- 580,718.51		--	-813,751.39
29- 3SBAL	150,000.00	100,000.00	- 50,000.00	100,000.00	--	100,000.00	--	100,000.00	--	- 50,000.00
30- CHBAL										
31- ESBAL										
32- GFBAL										
33- LSBAL	1,195,814.16	1,195,814.16	--	445,814.16	- 750,000.00	418,499.15	- 27,315.01	525,975.17	+107,476.02	-669,838.99
34- MNBAL	100,000.00	50,000.00	- 50,000.00	50,000.00	--	50,000.00	--	50,000.00	--	- 50,000.00
35- PTBAL										
36- SVBAL										
37- USBAL	534,346.16	384,346.16	-150,000.00	384,346.16	--	384,346.16	--	384,346.16	--	-150,000.00
38- UTBAL	3,284,976.88	3,284,976.88	--	3,284,976.88	--	3,284,976.88	--	3,287,244.98	+ 2,268.10	+ 2,268.10
39- WSBAL	45,164.18	45,164.18	--	45,164.18	--	45,164.18	--	45,164.18	--	--
40- WTBAL										
41- TOBAL	$6,936,354.69	$6,586,354.69	-350,000.00	$5,582,906.13	-1,003,448.56	$4,974,872.61	- 608,033.52	$4,717,030.98	-257,841.63	-2,219,323.71

Appendix E-1

Summary of Results of Mail-time and In-transit Survey
2D lock-box (hypothetical data)

	Area O Ala & Miss	Area P Florida	Area Q Texas	Area R Ark & Okla	Area S Louisiana	Total
1- Items from this area in 2D-region sample	686	871	1,022	795	611	3,985
2- Total items in 2D-region sample	3,985	3,985	3,985	3,985	3,985	3,985
3- % of (1) in (2)	17.21%	21.86%	25.65%	19.95%	15.33%	100.00%
4- Total value of items from this area in sample	$26,150.32	$35,859.07	$44,988.44	$32,666.55	$26,169.13	$165,833.51
5- Average per item value (4)/(1)	38.12	41.17	44.02	41.09	42.83	41.61
6- Normal monthly 2D volume-items	42,500	42,500	42,500	42,500	42,500	42,500
7- % of normal monthly volume in sample (2)/(6)	9.376471%	9.376471%	9.376471%	9.376471%	9.376471%	9.376471%
8- Est. monthly value of items from this area (4)/(7)	$278,893.00	$382,437.00	$479,801.00	$348,349.00	$279,094.00	$1,768,614.00
9- Est. monthly number of items from this area (3)(6)	7,314	9,291	10,901	8,479	6,515	42,500
10-						
11- Mail time to 2D (days)	1.61	1.78	1.32	1.79	1.80	
12- In-transit time from 2D	1.89	1.86	1.59	1.93	1.81	
13-						
14- Mail time to 3B	2.98	2.22	2.72	3.07	2.66	
15- In-transit time from 3B	2.00	2.00	2.00	2.00	2.00	
16-						
17- Mail time to CH	2.05	2.01	1.90	2.08	2.01	
18- In-transit time from CH	2.00	1.97	2.00	2.00	2.00	
19-						
20- Mail time to GF	1.61	1.78	1.32	1.79	1.80	
21- In-transit time from GF	1.89	1.86	1.59	1.93	1.81	
22-						
23- Mail time to PT	2.67	1.88	2.38	2.91	2.52	
24- In-transit time from PT	2.00	1.82	2.00	2.00	2.00	
25-						
26- Mail time to US	3.62	4.05	2.90	3.11	3.01	
27- In-transit time from US	2.00	2.00	2.00	2.00	2.00	

Summary of Results of Mail-time and In-transit Survey
3B lock-box (hypothetical data)

	Area A New England (ex. S. Conn.)	Area F Upstate New York	Total
1- Items from this area in 3B-region sample	2,411	704	3,115
2- Total items in 3B-region sample	3,115	3,115	3,115
3- % of (1) in (2)	77.40%	22.60%	100.00%
4- Total value of items from this area in sample	$ 101,647.76	$ 29,497.60	$ 131,145.36
5- Average per item value (4)/(1)	$ 42.16	41.90	42.10
6- Normal monthly 3B volume-items	33,600	33,600	33,600
7- % of normal monthly volume in sample (2)/(6)	9.270833%	9.270833%	9.270833%
8- Est. monthly value of items from this area (4)/(7)	$1,096,425.00	$318,176.00	$ 1,414,601.00
9- Est. monthly number of items from this area (3)(6)	26,006	7,594	33,600
10-			
11- Mail time to 2D (days)	2.94	3.12	
12- In-transit time from 2D	2.00	2.00	
13-			
14- Mail time to 3B	1.38	1.94	
15- In-transit time from 3B	1.00	1.00	
16-			
17- Mail time to CH	2.54	2.01	
18- In-transit time from CH	2.00	2.00	
19-			
20- Mail time to GF	2.18	3.02	
21- In-transit time from GF	2.00	2.00	
22-			
23- Mail time to PT	1.81	2.04	
24- In-transit time from PT	2.00	2.00	
25-			
26- Mail time to US	4.85	3.92	
27- In-transit time from US	2.00	2.00	

Summary of Results of Mail-time and In-transit Survey
CH lock-box (hypothetical data)

	Area D Ohio	Area G Metro Chicago	Area H So.Ill.,Iowa & Indiana	Area I Michigan	Area J Wisconsin	Area L Tenn & Ky	Area T Mo,Kan,E.Col, Nebr. & Wyo	Area U Minn,ND,SD, Mont, Idaho	Total
1- Items from this area in CH-region sample	918	1,922	412	1,017	619	498	562	473	6,421
2- Total items in CH-region sample	6,421	6,421	6,421	6,421	6,421	6,421	6,421	6,421	6,421
3- % of (1) in (2)	14.30%	29.93%	6.42%	15.84%	9.64%	7.76%	8.75%	7.36%	100.00%
4- Total value of items from this area in sample	$ 38,537.64	$ 82,223.16	$ 17,740.72	$ 44,870.04	$ 24,741.43	$ 18,635.16	$ 23,103.82	$ 20,887.68	$ 270,739.65
5- Average per item value (4)/(1)	41.98	42.78	43.06	44.12	39.97	37.42	41.11	44.16	42.16
6- Normal monthly CH volume-items									73,000
7- % of normal monthly volume in sample (2)/(6)	8.79589%	8.79589%	8.79589%	8.79589%	8.79589%	8.79589%	8.79589%	8.79589%	8.79589%
8- Est. monthly value of items from this area (4)/(7)	$ 438,132.00	$ 934,791.00	$ 201,693.00	$ 510,125.00	$ 281,284.00	$ 211,862.00	$ 262,666.00	$ 237,471.00	$3,078,024.00
9- Est. monthly number of items from this area (3)(6)	10,439	21,849	4,687	11,563	7,037	5,665	6,388	5,372	73,000
10-									
11- Mail time to 2D (days)	2.18	1.90	2.17	2.12	2.59	2.15	2.60	2.70	
12- In-transit time from 2D	2.00	2.00	2.00	2.00	2.00	2.00	2.00	2.00	
13-									
14- Mail time to 3B	1.99	1.96	2.40	1.89	2.05	2.32	3.89	2.99	
15- In-transit time from 3B	2.00	2.00	2.00	2.00	2.00	2.00	2.00	2.00	
16-									
17- Mail time to CH	1.60	.90	1.84	1.67	1.60	1.99	2.02	2.41	
18- In-transit time from CH	1.85	1.05	1.39	1.55	1.58	1.98	1.94	2.00	
19-									
20- Mail time to GF	1.82	2.50	2.59	2.14	2.81	1.39	2.98	3.15	
21- In-transit time from GF	2.00	2.00	2.00	2.00	2.00	1.82	2.00	2.00	
22-									
23- Mail time to PT	1.91	2.40	2.52	1.99	2.03	2.12	2.75	2.81	
24- In-transit time from PT	2.00	2.00	2.00	2.00	2.00	2.00	2.00	2.00	
25-									
26- Mail time to US	3.19	3.00	3.07	3.15	3.10	3.65	2.32	2.55	
27- In-transit time from US	2.00	2.00	2.00	2.00	2.00	2.00	2.00	2.00	

Summary of Results of Mail-time and In-transit Survey
PT lock-box (hypothetical data)

	Area B Metro NYC	Area C Mid Atlantic	Area E W. Pa. & W.Va.	Area K Virginia	Area M No.Carolina	Area N So.Car. & Ga.	Total
1- Items from this area in PT-region sample	681	587	233	147	175	194	2,017
2- Total items in PT region sample	2,017	2,017	2,017	2,017	2,017	2,017	2,017
3- % of (1) in (2)	33.76%	29.10%	11.55%	7.29%	8.68%	9.62%	100.00%
4- Total value of items from this area in sample	$ 28,029.96	$ 23,873.29	$ 9,063.70	$ 6,185.76	$ 6,856.50	$ 7,273.06	$ 81,282.27
5- Average per item value (4)/(1)	41.16	40.67	38.90	42.08	39.18	37.49	40.30
6- Normal monthly PT volume-items	23,800	23,800	23,800	23,800	23,800	23,800	23,800
7- % of normal monthly volume in sample (2)/(6)	8.4747489%	8.4747489%	8.4747489	8.4747489%	8.4747489%	8.4747489%	8.4747489%
8- Est. monthly value of items from this area (4)/(7)	$ 330,745.00	$ 286,061.00	$ 106,949.00	$ 72,990.00	$ 80,905.00	$ 85,820.00	$ 962,470.00
9- Est. monthly number of items from this area (3)(6)	8,035	6,926	2,749	1,735	2,066	2,289	23,800
10-							
11- Mail time to 2D (days)	2.41	2.36	2.72	2.42	2.32	2.45	
12- In-transit time from 2D	2.00	2.00	2.00	2.00	2.00	2.00	
13-							
14- Mail time to 3B	1.42	1.62	2.01	1.97	2.04	2.15	
15- In-transit time from 3B	1.85	2.00	2.00	2.00	2.00	2.00	
16-							
17- Mail time to CH	2.20	2.40	2.10	2.07	2.11	2.52	
18- In-transit time from CH	2.00	2.00	2.00	2.00	2.00	2.00	
19-							
20- Mail time to GF	2.35	1.81	2.01	1.82	1.76	1.72	
21- In-transit time from GF	2.00	1.92	1.90	1.81	1.61	1.31	
22-							
23- Mail time to PT	1.31	1.02	1.81	1.81	1.98	2.01	
24- In-transit time from PT	1.80	1.13	1.99	1.82	2.00	2.00	
25-							
26- Mail time to US	3.78	3.90	4.12	3.65	4.10	4.19	
27- In-transit time from US	2.00	2.00	2.00	2.00	2.00	2.00	

Summary of Results of Mail-time and In-transit Survey
US lock-box (hypothetical data)

	Area V Wash. & Ore.	Area W N. Cal.,Nevada, Utah,W.Colorado	Area X S.Cal., NM, Arizona	Total
1- Items from this area in US-region sample	687	1,502	2,619	4,808
2- Total items in CH-region sample	4,808	4,808	4,808	4,808
3- % of (1) in (2)	14.29%	31.24%	54.47%	100.00%
4- Total value of items from this area in sample	$ 30,310.44	66,869.04	118,352.61	215,532.09
5- Average per item value (4)/(1)	44.12	44.52	45.19	44.83
6- Normal monthly US volume-items	55,100	55,100	55,100	55,100
7- % of normal monthly volume in sample (2)/(6)	8.725952%	8.725952%	8.725952%	8.725952%
8- Est. monthly value of items from this area (4)/(7)	$ 347,360.00	$ 766,324.00	$ 1,356,328.00	$ 2,470,012.00
9- Est. monthly number of items from this area (3)(6)	7,874	17,213	30,013	55,100
10-				
11- Mail time to 2D (days)	2.98	2.82	2.65	
12- In-transit time from 2D	2.00	2.00	2.00	
13-				
14- Mail time to 3B	4.89	4.19	4.52	
15- In-transit time from 3B	2.00	2.00	2.00	
16-				
17- Mail time to CH	3.51	3.02	2.80	
18- In-transit time from CH	2.00	2.00	2.00	
19-				
20- Mail time to GF	4.52	4.19	4.11	
21- In-transit time from GF	2.00	2.00	2.00	
22-				
23- Mail time to PT	4.11	3.84	3.89	
24- In-transit time from PT	2.00	2.00	2.00	
25-				
26- Mail time to US	2.15	1.82	1.34	
27- In-transit time from US	1.89	1.79	1.14	

Appendix F.1.

AVERAGE BANK BALANCES - JULY 67 - $K

	BOOK BALANCE	FLOAT GEN BY DIS	GROSS BANK BALANCE	LESS CHECKS IN TRANSIT	NET COL BALANCE
2ND NATL NYC	51	3120	3171	0	3171
WALL ST TRUST NYC	3282	1536	4818	831	3987
MERCHANTS NATL NYC	1202	557	1759	0	1759
SUBTOTAL HQ BANKS	4535	5213	9748	831	8917
NATL BANK OF CHICAGO	811	112	923	372	551
LASALLE ST TRUST CHI	9	889	898	351	547
2ND NATL DALLAS	11	969	980	109	871
3RD NATL SOUTH BEND	250	0	250	0	250
SUBTOTAL CHI AC	1081	1970	3051	832	2219
3RD NATL BOSTON	565	0	565	64	501
WILLIAMS TRUST BOS	45	244	289	184	105
PHILADELPHIA TRUST	14	69	83	53	30
ELM ST TRUST N HAVEN	145	4	149	0	149
SUBTOTAL BOS AC	769	317	1086	301	785
US NATL SAN FRAN	19	722	741	227	514
UNION TRUST LA	534	0	534	179	355
SUNNYVILLE TRUST	100	0	100	0	100
SUBTOTAL SF AC	653	722	1375	406	969
TOTAL	7038	8222	15260	2370	12890

CHANGE IN AVERAGE BANK BALANCES - JULY 67 - $K

	NET COL BALANCE	CHANGE FROM LAST MONTH	CHANGE FROM SIX MO AVG
2ND NATL NYC	3171	+ 82	+ 39
WALL ST TRUST NYC	3987	- 42	- 12
MERCHANTS NATL NYC	1759	+ 7	- 7
SUBTOTAL HQ BANKS	8917	+ 47	+ 20
NATL BANK OF CHICAGO	551	- 12	- 3
LAS/LLE ST TRUST CHI	547	- 5	- 7
2ND NATL DALLAS	871	- 2	- 1
3RD NATL SOUTH BEND	250	0	+ 1
SUBTOTAL CHI AC	2219	- 19	- 10
3RD NATL BOSTON	501	+ 1	- 9
WILLIAMS TRUST BOS	105	- 7	- 6
PHILADELPHIA TRUST	30	- 12	- 2
ELM ST TRUST N HAVEN	149	0	- 1
SUBTOTAL BOS AC	785	- 18	- 18
US NATL SAN FRAN	514	+ 7	+ 1
UNION TRUST LA	355	+ 1	- 6
SUNNYVILLE TRUST	100	0	+ 2
SUBTOTAL SF AC	969	+ 8	- 3
TOTAL	12890	+ 18	- 11

TAX PAYMENT REPORT - JULY 67 - $K

	SERVICE CHARGE CREDIT OBTAINED	NO SERVICE CHARGE CREDIT VALUE	TOTAL
2ND NATL NYC	0	513	513
WALL ST TRUST NYC	0	500	500
MERCHANTS NATL NYC	0	500	500
SUBTOTAL HQ BANKS	0	1513	1513
NATL BANK OF CHICAGO	527	0	527
LASALLE TRUST CHI	0	0	0
2ND NATL DALLAS	0	0	0
3RD NATL SOUTH BEND			
SUBTOTAL CHI AC	527	0	527
3RD NATL BOSTON	401	0	401
WILLIAMS TRUST BOS	190	0	190
PHILADELPHIA TRUST	599	0	599
ELM ST TRUST N HAVEN	0	0	0
SUBTOTAL BOST AC	1190	0	1190
US NATL SAN FRAN	711	0	711
UNION TRUST LA	0	0	0
SUNNYVILLE TRUST	0	0	0
SUBTOTAL SF AC	711	0	711
TOTAL	2428	1513	3941

LOCK BOX COLLECTION COSTS - JULY 67

COMPARISON OF RLB COSTS

	CASH FEE PER ITEM	NCB REQ FOR ONE RLB ITEM	TAX REQ FOR ONE RLB ITEM	FEE-EQUIV ANAL CHARGE*	MRG COST PER ITEM
NATL BANK OF CHICAGO	3.75C	$10.52	$18.47	3.61C	2.51C
2ND NATL DALLAS	NA	$17.96	NA	6.02C	27.14C
3RD NATL BOSTON	NA	$18.00	$32.72	6.03C	.03C
PHILADELPHIA TRUST	4.38C	$12.00	$24.01	4.02C	.02C
US NATL SAN FRAN	4.42C	$12.61	$32.57	4.23C	2.96C
UNWEIGHTED AVERAGE	4.18C	$14.22	$26.94	4.78C	6.53C

COMPARISON OF WLB COSTS

	CASH FEE PER ITEM	NCB REQ FOR ONE WLB ITEM	TAX REQ FOR ONE WLB ITEM	FEE-EQUIV ANAL CHARGE*	MRG COST PER ITEM
NATL BANK OF CHICAGO	6.5C	$18.23	$32.02	6.27C	4.34C
LASALLE ST TRUST CHI	NA	$28.74	$53.88	9.63C	0
WILLIAMS TRUST BOS	NA	$26.06	$52.11	8.74C	21.75C
US NATL SAN FRAN	8.06C	$23.00	$59.39	7.71C	5.39C
UNION TRUST LA	NA	$28.74	NA	9.63C	0
UNWEIGHTED AVERAGE	7.28C	$24.95	$49.35	8.40C	6.30C

* AFI FUNDS VALUED AT (5.125PC)(.94) OR 4.8175PC

XY BANK - JULY 67

	FEB	MAR	APR	MAY	JUN	JUL	6 MØ AVG
AVG BK BAL $K	460	453	450	463	512	541	480
+ FLØAT $K	309	316	311	314	299	312	310
GR BANKBAL $K	769	769	761	777	811	853	790
-INTRANSIT $K	285	289	278	272	281	297	284
NT CØL BAL $K	484	480	483	505	530	556	506
TAX PYMNTS $K	600	750	620	575	575	400	587
AVG LØANS $K	1561	1557	1554	1707	1870	2033	2033
NCB/AVG LØANS	31.0PC	30.8PC	31.1PC	29.6PC	28.3PC	27.3PC	24.9PC
CXP	286	298	282	301	288	290	291
RLB	33841	35622	32980	32007	34012	31113	33263
WLB	5112	5723	5019	5788	5223	5001	5311
ØMC	$ 88.50	$ 92.00	$ 97.25	$ 91.25	$ 95.00	$ 89.75	$ 92.29
MUC	$ 0	$ 15.41	$ 3.52	$ 0	$ 0	$ 0	$ 3.16
MUK	$ 0	$ 0	$ 0	$ 5.93	$ 4.67	$ 11.49	$ 3.68
TVL	$1358.22	$1487.91	$1373.70	$1369.12	$1410.79	$1293.65	$1382.23
CST	$1373.63	$1491.43	$1367.77	$1364.45	$1399.30	$1288.70	$1380.88
TVL-CST	$ 15.41-	$ 3.52-	$ 5.93	$ 4.67	$ 11.49	$ 4.95	$ 1.35
TVL (CH)	$2946.48	$3234.14	$2980.98	$2968.08	$3057.23	$2794.70	$2996.94
CST (CH)	$1704.12	$1830.14	$1677.86	$1676.85	$1719.68	$1584.57	$1698.87
TVL-CST(CH)	$1242.36	$1404.04	$1303.12	$1291.23	$1337.55	$1210.13	$1298.07

REVENUE AND CØST FACTORS - JULY 67

	XY	CH	8 BANKS		XY	CH	8 BANKS
VNB	0.001667	0.003566	0.002495	NCB/RLB	$18.00	$10.52	$14.22
VTP	0.000917	0.00203	0.00128	TAX/RLB	$32.72	$18.47	$26.94
CXP	0.05	0.05	0.0481	NCB/WLB	$31.49	$18.23	$24.95
CXD	0.03	0.02	0.0233	TAX/WLB	$57.25	$32.02	$49.35
RLB	0.03	0.0375	0.0363				
WLB	0.0525	0.065	0.062				

List of Mnemonic Symbols Used in CASH ALPHA

First-two digits

2D	Second National Bank of Dallas
2Y	Second National Bank, New York
3B	Third National Bank of Boston
3S	Third National Bank of South Bend
BA	Boston Accounting Center
CA	Chicago Accounting Center
CH	National Bank of Chicago
ES	Elm Street Trust Company, New Haven
GF	Georgia-First National Bank, Atlanta
HQ	New York Headquarters - Unallocated Variables
LS	LaSalle Street Trust Company, Chicago
MN	Merchants National Bank, New York
NG	Negotiated tax - used in Alternate 1
NY	New York Headquarters
PT	Philadelphia Trust Company
SF	San Francisco Accounting Center
SV	Sunnyville Trust Company
TO	Total
US	U.S. National Bank of California
UT	Union Trust Company, Los Angeles
WS	Wall Street Trust Company
WT	Williams Trust Company, Boston

Last-three digits

ARL	RLB items handled per month from Area A
BAL	Company cash book balances, monthly average
BRL	RLB items handled per month from Area B
CRL	RLB items handled per month from Area C
CST	Total activity costs from bank analysis for month
CTN	Checks in transit, monthly average
CXD	Number of checks deposited during month
CXP	Number of checks paid during month
DEP	Deposits during month
DIS	General disbursements during month
DIV	Dividend disbursements during month (6-month moving average)
DRL	RLB items handled per month from Area D
ERL	RLB items handled per month from Area E
FEE	Cash fee paid
FRL	RLB items handled per month from Area F

GRL   RLB items handled per month from Area G
HQD   General disbursements made by NY during month
HRL   RLB items handled per month from Area H

IDS   Ancama International's monthly disbursements
IRL   RLB items handled per month from Area I
JRL   RLB items handled per month from Area J

KRL   RLB items handled per month from Area K
LNS   Loan balance, all loans, 6-month moving average
LNU   Lines unused, 6-month moving average

LRL   RLB items handled per month from Area L
MRL   RLB items handled per month from Area M
MUC   Make-up costs, cumulative from prior months

MUK   Make-up credits, cumulative from prior months
NCB   Net collected balances, monthly average
NRL   RLB items handled per month from Area N

OMC   Other monthly costs - $ m
ORL   RLB items handled per month from Area O
OTC   Over-the-counter deposits during month

PAY   Payroll disbursements during month
PRL   RLB items handled per month from Area P
QRL   RLB items handled per month from Area Q

RCV   Average investments in RLB receivables from mailing to collection
RLB   Retail lock-box items handled during month
RRL   RLB items handled per month from Area R

SRL   RLB items handled per month from Area S
TAX   Tax payments made during month
TRL   RLB items handled per month from Area T

TVL   Total value of compensation to bank
URL   RLB items handled per month from Area U
VNB   Value of net collected balances to bank

VRL   RLB items handled per month from Area V
VTP   Value of tax payments to bank
WLB   Wholesale lock-box items handled during month

WRL   RLB items handled per month from Area W
WSD   Wholesale lock-box items handled during month
XRL   RLB items handled per month from Area X

CASH ALPHA Equation Listing

(Note: This appendix contains the equations that were used in the
five CASH ALPHA cases. The equation listing is somewhat more complex than would be necessary in an ongoing system, as for this study
all five cases were processed in one computer run.)

EQUATION	0	IS	000
RHS			FUNCT
1	-	0.00001	HQHQD
2	-	0.00001	HQTAX
3	+	10.0	NGTAX
4	+	0.016667	TOBAL
5	+	1.0	TOFEE
6	+	0.016667	TORCV
7	+	10.0	52DACT

EQUATION	1	IS	001
RHS			FUNCT
1	-	0.00001	HQHQD
2	-	0.00001	HQTAX
3	+	0.016667	TOBAL
4	+	1.0	TOFEE
5	+	0.016667	TORCV
6	+	10.0	52DACT

EQUATION	2	IS	002
RHS			FUNCT
1	-	0.00001	HQHQD
2	-	0.00001	HQTAX
3	+	0.016667	TOBAL
4	+	1.0	TOFEE
5	+	0.016667	TORCV

EQUATION	3	IS	010
RHS			FUNCT
1	-	1.0	TOBAL
2	-	1.0	TORCV

EQUATION	4	IS	2DCST
RHS	+	0.0	EQUAL
1	-	1.0	2DCST
2	+	0.06	2DCXP
3	+	1.0	2DMUC
4	-	1.0	2DMUK
5	+	1.0	2DOMC
6	+	0.045	2DRLB
7	+	0.05	52DCXP
8	+	0.0375	52DRLB

EQUATION	5	IS	2DCTN
RHS	+	0.0	EQUAL
1	-	2.77	2DARL
2	-	2.7	2DBRL
3	-	2.67	2DCRL
4	+	1.0	2DCTN
5	-	0.059244	2DDEP
6	-	2.76	2DDRL
7	-	2.56	2DERL
8	-	2.75	2DFRL
9	-	2.81	2DGRL
10	-	2.83	2DHRL
11	-	2.9	2DIRL
12	-	2.63	2DJRL
13	-	2.77	2DKRL
14	-	2.46	2DLRL
15	-	2.58	2DMRL
16	-	2.46	2DNRL
17	-	2.37	2DORL
18	-	2.52	2DPRL
19	-	2.3	2DQRL
20	-	2.6	2DRRL
21	-	2.55	2DSRL
22	-	2.7	2DTRL
23	-	2.9	2DURL
24	-	2.9	2DVRL
25	-	2.93	2DWRL
26	-	2.97	2DXRL

EQUATION	6	IS	2DCXP
RHS	+	0.0	EQUAL
1	+	1.0	2DCXP
2	-	0.000517	2DDIS
3	+	1.0	52DCXP

EQUATION	7	IS	2DDEP
RHS	+	1.769	EQUAL
1	+	1.0	2DDEP

EQUATION	8	IS	2DFEE
RHS	+	0.0	LESS
1	-	0.333333	2DTVL
2	+	1.0	52DFEE

EQUATION 9 IS 2DMUC
RHS + 0.0 EQUAL

| 1 | + | 1.0 | 2DMUC |
| 2 | - | 1.0 | 2DMUK |

EQUATION 10 IS 2DNCB
RHS + 0.0 EQUAL

1	+	1.0	2DBAL
2	-	1.0	2DCTN
3	+	0.22593	2DDIS
4	-	1.0	2DNCB
5	-	1.0	52DNCB

EQUATION 11 IS 2DOMC
RHS + 0.000125 EQUAL

| 1 | + | 1.0 | 2DOMC |
| 2 | + | 1.0 | 52DOMC |

EQUATION 12 IS 2DRCV
RHS + 0.0 EQUAL

1	+	4.07	2DARL
2	+	3.26	2DBRL
3	+	3.15	2DCRL
4	+	3.01	2DDRL
5	+	3.48	2DERL
6	+	4.3	2DFRL
7	+	2.67	2DGRL
8	+	3.07	2DHRL
9	+	3.07	2DIRL
10	+	3.4	2DJRL
11	+	3.35	2DKRL
12	+	2.64	2DLRL
13	+	2.99	2DMRL
14	+	3.02	2DNRL
15	+	2.02	2DORL
16	+	2.41	2DPRL
17	+	1.91	2DQRL
18	-	1.0	2DRCV
19	+	2.42	2DRRL
20	+	2.53	2DSRL
21	+	3.51	2DTRL
22	+	3.92	2DURL
23	+	4.32	2DVRL
24	+	4.13	2DWRL
25	+	3.94	2DXRL

EQUATION 13 IS 2DRLB
RHS + 0.0425 EQUAL

1	-	1.0	2DARL
2	-	1.0	2DBRL
3	-	1.0	2DCRL
4	-	1.0	2DDRL
5	-	1.0	2DERL
6	-	1.0	2DFRL
7	-	1.0	2DGRL
8	-	1.0	2DHRL
9	-	1.0	2DIRL
10	-	1.0	2DJRL
11	-	1.0	2DKRL
12	-	1.0	2DLRL
13	-	1.0	2DMRL
14	-	1.0	2DNRL
15	-	1.0	2DORL
16	-	1.0	2DPRL
17	-	1.0	2DQRL
18	+	1.0	2DRLB
19	-	1.0	2DRRL
20	-	1.0	2DSRL
21	-	1.0	2DTRL
22	-	1.0	2DURL
23	-	1.0	2DVRL
24	-	1.0	2DWRL
25	-	1.0	2DXRL
26	+	1.0	52DRLB

EQUATION 14 IS 2DTVL
RHS + 0.0 EQUAL

1	-	1.0	2DTVL
2	+	1.0	2DVNB
3	+	1.0	2DVTP
4	+	1.0	52DFEE

EQUATION 15 IS 2DVNB
RHS + 0.0 EQUAL

1	+	0.002505	2DNCB
2	-	1.0	2DVNB
3	+	0.003566	52DNCB

EQUATION 16 IS 2DVTP
RHS + 0.0 EQUAL

| 1 | - | 1.0 | 2DVTP |
| 2 | + | 0.00203 | 52DTAX |

EQUATION	17	IS	2YCST
RHS +	0.0		EQUAL
1 -	1.0		2YCST
2 +	0.05		2YCXP
3 +	0.05		2YDXP
4 +	1.0		2YMUC
5 -	1.0		2YMUK
6 +	1.0		2YOMC

EQUATION	18	IS	2YCTN
RHS +	0.0		EQUAL
1 +	1.0		2YCTN

EQUATION	19	IS	2YCXP
RHS +	0.0		EQUAL
1 +	1.0		2YCXP
2 -	0.00034		2YDIS
3 -	0.004973		2YDIV
4 -	0.00034		2YHQD

EQUATION	20	IS	2YDIV
RHS +	0.75		EQUAL
1 +	1.0		2YDIV

EQUATION	21	IS	2YDXP
RHS +	0.0112		EQUAL
1 +	1.0		2YDXP

EQUATION	22	IS	2YHQD
RHS +	0.0		GREATE
1 +	1.0		2YHQD
2 -	0.2		NYHQD

EQUATION	23	IS	2YLNS
RHS +	7.1		EQUAL
1 +	1.0		2YLNS

EQUATION	24	IS	2YLNU
RHS +	5.0		EQUAL
1 +	1.0		2YLNU

EQUATION	25	IS	2YMUC
RHS +	0.0		EQUAL
1 +	1.0		2YMUC
2 -	1.0		2YMUK

EQUATION	26	IS	2YNCB
RHS +	0.0		EQUAL
1 +	1.0		2YBAL
2 -	1.0		2YCTN
3 +	0.20594		2YDIS
4 +	0.253333		2YDIV
5 +	0.2127		2YHQD
6 -	1.0		2YNCB

EQUATION	27	IS	2YOMC
RHS +	0.00001		EQUAL
1 +	1.0		2YOMC

EQUATION	28	IS	2YVNB
RHS +	0.0		EQUAL
1 +	0.003566		2YNCB
2 -	1.0		2YVNB

EQUATION	29	IS	3BCST
RHS +	0.0		EQUAL
1 -	1.0		3BCST
2 +	0.03		3BCXD
3 +	0.05		3BCXP
4 +	1.0		3BMUC
5 -	1.0		3BMUK
6 +	1.0		3BOMC
7 +	0.03		3BRLB

```
EQUATION    30  IS  3BCTN
RHS  +      0.0     EQUAL

 1 -    1.39        3BARL
 2 -    2.5         3BBRL
 3 -    2.67        3BCRL
 4 +    1.0         3BCTN
 5 -    0.032877    3BDEP
 6 -    2.76        3BDRL
 7 -    2.56        3BERL
 8 -    1.38        3BFRL
 9 -    2.81        3BGRL
10 -    2.83        3BHRL
11 -    2.9         3BIRL
12 -    2.63        3BJRL
13 -    2.77        3BKRL
14 -    2.46        3BLRL
15 -    2.58        3BMRL
16 -    2.46        3BNRL
17 -    2.5         3BORL
18 -    0.032877    3BOTC
19 -    2.7         3BPRL
20 -    2.9         3BQRL
21 -    2.7         3BRRL
22 -    2.82        3BSRL
23 -    2.7         3BTRL
24 -    2.9         3BURL
25 -    2.9         3BVRL
26 -    2.9         3BWRL
27 -    2.97        3BXRL


EQUATION    31  IS  3BCXD
RHS  +      0.00154 EQUAL

 1 +    1.0         3BCXD


EQUATION    32  IS  3BCXP
RHS  +      0.0     EQUAL

 1 +    1.0         3BCXP
 2 -    0.002709    3BDIS


EQUATION    33  IS  3BDEP
RHS  +      1.895   EQUAL

 1 +    1.0         3BDEP


EQUATION    34  IS  3BMUC
RHS  +      0.0     EQUAL

 1 +    1.0         3BMUC
 2 -    1.0         3BMUK


EQUATION    35  IS  3BNCB
RHS  +      0.0     EQUAL

 1 +    1.0         3BBAL
 2 -    1.0         3BCTN
 3 +    0.18189     3BDIS
 4 -    1.0         3BNCB


EQUATION    36  IS  3BOMC
RHS  +      0.000145 EQUAL

 1 +    1.0         3BOMC


EQUATION    37  IS  3BOTC
RHS  +      0.0     EQUAL

 1 +    1.0         3BOTC


EQUATION    38  IS  3BRCV
RHS  +      0.0     EQUAL

 1 +    1.91        3BARL
 2 +    1.92        3BBRL
 3 +    2.16        3BCRL
 4 +    2.75        3BDRL
 5 +    2.57        3BERL
 6 +    2.67        3BFRL
 7 +    2.76        3BGRL
 8 +    3.4         3BHRL
 9 +    2.74        3BIRL
10 +    2.69        3BJRL
11 +    2.72        3BKRL
12 +    2.85        3BLRL
13 +    2.62        3BMRL
14 +    2.65        3BNRL
15 +    3.73        3BORL
16 +    3.0         3BPRL
17 +    3.93        3BQRL
18 -    1.0         3BRCV
19 +    4.15        3BRRL
20 +    3.74        3BSRL
21 +    5.25        3BTRL
22 +    4.34        3BURL
23 +    7.1         3BVRL
24 +    6.13        3BWRL
25 +    6.7         3BXRL
```

EQUATION	39	IS	3BRLB
RHS +	0.0336		EQUAL

1 -	1.0	3BARL
2 -	1.0	3BBRL
3 -	1.0	3BCRL
4 -	1.0	3BDRL
5 -	1.0	3BERL
6 -	1.0	3BFRL
7 -	1.0	3BGRL
8 -	1.0	3BHRL
9 -	1.0	3BIRL
10 -	1.0	3BJRL
11 -	1.0	3BKRL
12 -	1.0	3BLRL
13 -	1.0	3BMRL
14 -	1.0	3BNRL
15 -	1.0	3BORL
16 -	1.0	3BPRL
17 -	1.0	3BQRL
18 +	1.0	3BRLB
19 -	1.0	3BRRL
20 -	1.0	3BSRL
21 -	1.0	3BTRL
22 -	1.0	3BURL
23 -	1.0	3BVRL
24 -	1.0	3BWRL
25 -	1.0	3BXRL

EQUATION	40	IS	3BTVL
RHS +	0.0		EQUAL

1 -	1.0	3BTVL
2 +	1.0	3BVNB
3 +	1.0	3BVTP

EQUATION	41	IS	3BVNB
RHS +	0.0		EQUAL

1 +	0.001667	3BNCB
2 -	1.0	3BVNB

EQUATION	42	IS	3BVTP
RHS +	0.0		EQUAL

1 +	0.000917	3BTAX
2 -	1.0	3BVTP

EQUATION	43	IS	3SNCB
RHS +	0.0		EQUAL

1 +	1.0	3SBAL
2 -	1.0	3SNCB

EQUATION	44	IS	3STAX
RHS +	0.2		LESS

1 +	1.0	43STAX

EQUATION	45	IS	BADIS
RHS +	1.89		EQUAL

1 +	1.0	3BDIS
2 +	1.0	MNDIS
3 +	1.0	PTDIS

EQUATION	46	IS	CADIS
RHS +	9.6		EQUAL

1 +	1.0	2DDIS
2 +	1.0	2YDIS
3 +	1.0	CHDIS
4 +	1.0	GFDIS
5 +	1.0	LSDIS

EQUATION	47	IS	CHCST
RHS +	0.0		EQUAL

1 -	1.0	CHCST
2 +	0.02	CHCXD
3 +	0.05	CHCXP
4 +	1.0	CHMUC
5 -	1.0	CHMUK
6 +	1.0	CHOMC
7 +	0.0375	CHRLB
8 +	0.065	CHWLB

130

EQUATION 48 IS CHCTN
RHS + 0.0 EQUAL

1	-	2.77	CHARL
2	-	2.7	CHBRL
3	-	2.67	CHCRL
4	+	1.0	CHCTN
5	-	0.05063	CHDEP
6	-	2.55	CHDRL
7	-	2.56	CHERL
8	-	2.77	CHFRL
9	-	1.48	CHGRL
10	-	1.97	CHHRL
11	-	2.25	CHIRL
12	-	2.07	CHJRL
13	-	2.77	CHKRL
14	-	2.44	CHLRL
15	-	2.58	CHMRL
16	-	2.46	CHNRL
17	-	2.5	CHORL
18	-	0.05063	CHOTC
19	-	2.68	CHPRL
20	-	2.9	CHQRL
21	-	2.7	CHRRL
22	-	2.82	CHSRL
23	-	2.62	CHTRL
24	-	2.9	CHURL
25	-	2.9	CHVRL
26	-	2.93	CHWRL
27	-	0.05063	CHWSD
28	-	2.97	CHXRL

EQUATION 49 IS CHCXD
RHS + 0.0007 EQUAL

1	+	1.0	CHCXD

EQUATION 50 IS CHCXP
RHS + 0.0 EQUAL

1	+	1.0	CHCXP
2	-	0.000517	CHDIS

EQUATION 51 IS CHDEP
RHS + 7.328 EQUAL

1	+	1.0	CHDEP

EQUATION 52 IS CHFEE
RHS + 0.0 LESS

1	+	1.0	CHFEE
2	-	0.333333	CHTVL

EQUATION 53 IS CHLNS
RHS + 0.35 EQUAL

1	+	1.0	CHLNS

EQUATION 54 IS CHMUC
RHS + 0.0 EQUAL

1	+	1.0	CHMUC
2	-	1.0	CHMUK

EQUATION 55 IS CHNCB
RHS + 0.0 EQUAL

1	+	1.0	CHBAL
2	-	1.0	CHCTN
3	+	0.19459	CHDIS
4	-	1.0	CHNCB

EQUATION 56 IS CHOMC
RHS + 0.00009 EQUAL

1	+	1.0	CHOMC

EQUATION 57 IS CHOTC
RHS + 0.0 EQUAL

1	+	1.0	CHOTC

EQUATION 58 IS CHRCV
RHS + 0.0 EQUAL

1	+	3.52	CHARL
2	+	2.97	CHBRL
3	+	3.21	CHCRL
4	+	2.21	CHDRL
5	+	2.68	CHERL
6	+	2.76	CHFRL
7	+	1.27	CHGRL
8	+	2.61	CHHRL
9	+	2.42	CHIRL
10	+	2.1	CHJRL
11	+	2.86	CHKRL
12	+	2.44	CHLRL
13	+	2.72	CHMRL
14	+	3.11	CHNRL
15	+	2.57	CHORL
16	+	2.72	CHPRL
17	+	2.75	CHQRL
18	-	1.0	CHRCV
19	+	2.81	CHRRL
20	+	2.83	CHSRL
21	+	2.73	CHTRL
22	+	3.49	CHURL
23	+	5.09	CHVRL
24	+	4.42	CHWRL
25	+	4.16	CHXRL

EQUATION	59	IS	CHRLB
RHS +	0.073		EQUAL

1 −	1.0		CHARL
2 −	1.0		CHBRL
3 −	1.0		CHCRL
4 −	1.0		CHDRL
5 −	1.0		CHERL
6 −	1.0		CHFRL
7 −	1.0		CHGRL
8 −	1.0		CHHRL
9 −	1.0		CHIRL
10 −	1.0		CHJRL
11 −	1.0		CHKRL
12 −	1.0		CHLRL
13 −	1.0		CHMRL
14 −	1.0		CHNRL
15 −	1.0		CHORL
16 −	1.0		CHPRL
17 −	1.0		CHQRL
18 +	1.0		CHRLB
19 −	1.0		CHRRL
20 −	1.0		CHSRL
21 −	1.0		CHTRL
22 −	1.0		CHURL
23 −	1.0		CHVRL
24 −	1.0		CHWRL
25 −	1.0		CHXRL

EQUATION	60	IS	CHTVL
RHS +	0.0		EQUAL

1 +	1.0		CHFEE
2 −	1.0		CHTVL
3 +	1.0		CHVNB
4 +	1.0		CHVTP

EQUATION	61	IS	CHVNB
RHS +	0.0		EQUAL

1 +	0.003566		CHNCB
2 −	1.0		CHVNB

EQUATION	62	IS	CHVTP
RHS +	0.0		EQUAL

1 +	0.00203		CHTAX
2 −	1.0		CHVTP

EQUATION	63	IS	CHWLB
RHS +	0.0051		EQUAL

1 +	1.0		CHWLB

EQUATION	64	IS	CHWSD
RHS +	0.0		EQUAL

1 +	1.0		CHWSD

EQUATION	65	IS	ESNCB
RHS +	0.0		EQUAL

1 +	1.0		ESBAL
2 −	1.0		ESNCB

EQUATION	66	IS	ESTAX
RHS +	0.1		LESS

1 +	1.0		4ESTAX

EQUATION	67	IS	GFCST
RHS +	0.0		EQUAL

1 −	1.0		GFCST
2 +	0.05		GFCXP
3 +	1.0		GFMUC
4 −	1.0		GFMUK
5 +	1.0		GFOMC
6 +	0.0425		GFRLB

	EQUATION	68	IS	GFCTN
RHS	+	0.0		EQUAL
1	+	2.77		GFARL
2	+	2.7		GFBRL
3	+	2.56		GFCRL
4	−	1.0		GFCTN
5	+	2.76		GFDRL
6	+	2.43		GFERL
7	+	2.75		GFFRL
8	+	2.81		GFGRL
9	+	2.83		GFHRL
10	+	2.9		GFIRL
11	+	2.63		GFJRL
12	+	2.5		GFKRL
13	+	2.24		GFLRL
14	+	2.08		GFMRL
15	+	1.61		GFNRL
16	+	2.25		GFORL
17	+	2.32		GFPRL
18	+	2.9		GFQRL
19	+	2.7		GFRRL
20	+	2.68		GFSRL
21	+	2.7		GFTRL
22	+	2.9		GFURL
23	+	2.9		GFVRL
24	+	2.93		GFWRL
25	+	2.97		GFXRL

	EQUATION	69	IS	GFCXP
RHS	+	0.0		EQUAL
1	+	1.0		GFCXP
2	−	0.000517		GFDIS

	EQUATION	70	IS	GFDIS
RHS	+	0.0		LESS
1	+	1.0		GFDIS

	EQUATION	71	IS	GFMUC
RHS	+	0.0		EQUAL
1	+	1.0		GFMUC
2	−	1.0		GFMUK

	EQUATION	72	IS	GFNCB
RHS	+	0.0		EQUAL
1	+	1.0		GFBAL
2	−	1.0		GFCTN
3	+	0.20594		GFDIS
4	−	1.0		GFNCB

	EQUATION	73	IS	GFOMC
RHS	+	0.0		EQUAL
1	+	1.0		GFOMC

	EQUATION	74	IS	GFRCV
RHS	+	0.0		EQUAL
1	+	3.05		GFARL
2	+	3.17		GFBRL
3	+	2.42		GFCRL
4	+	2.51		GFDRL
5	+	2.57		GFERL
6	+	4.15		GFFRL
7	+	3.52		GFGRL
8	+	3.67		GFHRL
9	+	3.1		GFIRL
10	+	3.69		GFJRL
11	+	2.52		GFKRL
12	+	1.71		GFLRL
13	+	2.26		GFMRL
14	+	2.12		GFNRL
15	+	2.16		GFORL
16	+	1.87		GFPRL
17	+	3.54		GFQRL
18	−	1.0		GFRCV
19	+	3.85		GFRRL
20	+	2.69		GFSRL
21	+	4.02		GFTRL
22	+	4.57		GFURL
23	+	6.55		GFVRL
24	+	6.14		GFWRL
25	+	6.1		GFXRL

EQUATION	75	IS	GFRLB
RHS	+	0.0	EQUAL

1	-	1.0	GFARL
2	-	1.0	GFBRL
3	-	1.0	GFCRL
4	-	1.0	GFDRL
5	-	1.0	GFERL
6	-	1.0	GFFRL
7	-	1.0	GFGRL
8	-	1.0	GFHRL
9	-	1.0	GFIRL
10	-	1.0	GFJRL
11	-	1.0	GFKRL
12	-	1.0	GFLRL
13	-	1.0	GFMRL
14	-	1.0	GFNRL
15	-	1.0	GFORL
16	-	1.0	GFPRL
17	-	1.0	GFQRL
18	+	1.0	GFRLB
19	-	1.0	GFRRL
20	-	1.0	GFSRL
21	-	1.0	GFTRL
22	-	1.0	GFURL
23	-	1.0	GFVRL
24	-	1.0	GFWRL
25	-	1.0	GFXRL

EQUATION	76	IS	GFVNB
RHS	+	0.0	EQUAL

1	+	0.0025	GFNCB
2	-	1.0	GFVNB

EQUATION	77	IS	LSCST
RHS	+	0.0	EQUAL

1	-	1.0	LSCST
2	+	0.035	LSCXP
3	+	1.0	LSMUC
4	-	1.0	LSMUK
5	-	1.0	LSOMC
6	+	0.05	LSWLB

EQUATION	78	IS	LSCTN
RHS	+	0.0	EQUAL

1	+	1.0	LSCTN
2	-	0.056877	LSDEP

EQUATION	79	IS	LSCXP
RHS	+	0.0	EQUAL

1	+	1.0	LSCXP
2	-	0.000517	LSDIS

EQUATION	80	IS	LSDEP
RHS	+	6.11	EQUAL

1	+	1.0	LSDEP

EQUATION	81	IS	LSLNS
RHS	+	0.35	EQUAL

1	+	1.0	LSLNS

EQUATION	'82	IS	LSMUC
RHS	+	0.0	EQUAL

1	+	1.0	LSMUC
2	-	1.0	LSMUK

EQUATION	83	IS	LSNCB
RHS	+	0.0	EQUAL

1	+	1.0	LSBAL
2	-	1.0	LSCTN
3	+	0.20377	LSDIS
4	-	1.0	LSNCB
5	+	0.15185	LSPAY

EQUATION	84	IS	LSOMC
RHS	+	0.0001	EQUAL

1	+	1.0	LSOMC

EQUATION	85	IS	LSPAY
RHS	+	4.32	EQUAL

1	+	1.0	LSPAY

EQUATION	86	IS	LSTVL
RHS	+	0.0	EQUAL

1	-	1.0	LSTVL
2	+	1.0	LSVNB
3	+	1.0	LSVTP

EQUATION	87	IS	LSVNB
RHS	+	0.0	EQUAL

1	+	0.00174	LSNCB
2	-	1.0	LSVNB

EQUATION	88	IS	LSVTP
RHS +	0.0		EQUAL

1 +	0.000928	LSTAX
2 −	1.0	LSVTP

EQUATION	89	IS	LSWLB
RHS +	0.0079		EQUAL

1 +	1.0	LSWLB

EQUATION	90	IS	MNCST
RHS +	0.0		EQUAL

1 −	1.0	MNCST
2 +	0.05	MNCXP
3 +	1.0	MNMUC
4 −	1.0	MNMUK
5 +	1.0	MNOMC

EQUATION	91	IS	MNCTN
RHS +	0.0		EQUAL

1 +	1.0	MNCTN

EQUATION	92	IS	MNCXP
RHS +	0.0		EQUAL

1 +	1.0	MNCXP
2 −	0.00034	MNDIS
3 −	0.00034	MNHQD

EQUATION	93	IS	MNHQD
RHS +	0.0		GREATE

1 +	1.0	MNHQD
2 −	0.1	NYHQD

EQUATION	94	IS	MNLNS
RHS +	3.05		EQUAL

1 +	1.0	MNLNS

EQUATION	95	IS	MNLNU
RHS +	3.0		EQUAL

1 +	1.0	MNLNU

EQUATION	96	IS	MNMUC
RHS +	0.0		EQUAL

1 +	1.0	MNMUC
2 −	1.0	MNMUK

EQUATION	97	IS	MNNCB
RHS +	0.0		EQUAL

1 +	1.0	MNBAL
2 −	1.0	MNCTN
3 +	0.18413	MNDIS
4 +	0.19828	MNHQD
5 −	1.0	MNNCB

EQUATION	98	IS	MNOMC
RHS +	0.002011		EQUAL

1 +	1.0	MNOMC

EQUATION	99	IS	MNVNB
RHS +	0.0		EQUAL

1 +	0.003566	MNNCB
2 −	1.0	MNVNB

EQUATION	100	IS	NGTAX
RHS +	0.0		EQUAL

1 −	1.0	NGTAX
2 +	1.0	43STAX
3 +	1.0	4ESTAX
4 +	1.0	4SVTAX
5 +	1.0	4UTTAX

EQUATION	101	IS	NYHQD
RHS +	0.0		EQUAL

1 +	1.0	2YHQD
2 +	1.0	HQHQD
3 +	1.0	MNHQD
4 −	1.0	NYHQD
5 +	1.0	WSHQD

EQUATION	102	IS	PTCST
RHS +	0.0		EQUAL

1 −	1.0	PTCST
2 +	0.05	PTCXP
3 +	1.0	PTMUC
4 −	1.0	PTMUK
5 +	1.0	PTOMC
6 +	0.035	PTRLB

EQUATION	103	IS	PTCTN
RHS +	0.0		EQUAL
1 −	2.77		PTARL
2 −	2.43		PTBRL
3 −	1.51		PTCRL
4 +	1.0		PTCTN
5 −	0.05474		PTDEP
6 −	2.76		PTDRL
7 −	2.54		PTERL
8 −	2.75		PTFRL
9 −	2.81		PTGRL
10 −	2.83		PTHRL
11 −	2.9		PTIRL
12 −	2.63		PTJRL
13 −	2.52		PTKRL
14 −	2.46		PTLRL
15 −	2.58		PTMRL
16 −	2.46		PTNRL
17 −	2.5		PTORL
18 −	2.46		PTPRL
19 −	2.9		PTQRL
20 −	2.7		PTRRL
21 −	2.82		PTSRL
22 −	2.7		PTTRL
23 −	2.9		PTURL
24 −	2.9		PTVRL
25 −	2.93		PTWRL
26 −	2.97		PTXRL

EQUATION	104	IS	PTCXP
RHS +	0.0		EQUAL
1 +	1.0		PTCXP
2 −	0.002709		PTDIS

EQUATION	105	IS	PTDEP
RHS +	0.962		EQUAL
1 +	1.0		PTDEP

EQUATION	106	IS	PTFEE
RHS +	0.0		GREATE
1 −	1.25		PTCST
2 +	1.0		PTFEE
3 +	1.25		PTVNB
4 +	1.25		PTVTP

EQUATION	107	IS	PTMUC
RHS +	0.0		EQUAL
1 +	1.0		PTMUC
2 −	1.0		PTMUK

EQUATION	108	IS	PTNCB
RHS +	0.0		EQUAL
1 +	1.0		PTBAL
2 −	1.0		PTCTN
3 +	0.18938		PTDIS
4 −	1.0		PTNCB

EQUATION	109	IS	PTOMC
RHS +	0.00004		EQUAL
1 +	1.0		PTOMC

EQUATION	110	IS	PTRCV
RHS +	0.0		EQUAL
1 +	2.51		PTARL
2 +	1.77		PTBRL
3 +	1.36		PTCRL
4 +	2.64		PTDRL
5 +	2.31		PTERL
6 +	2.81		PTFRL
7 +	3.37		PTGRL
8 +	3.57		PTHRL
9 +	2.88		PTIRL
10 +	2.67		PTJRL
11 +	2.5		PTKRL
12 +	2.61		PTLRL
13 +	2.55		PTMRL
14 +	2.48		PTNRL
15 +	3.35		PTORL
16 +	2.54		PTPRL
17 +	3.44		PTQRL
18 −	1.0		PTRCV
19 +	3.93		PTRRL
20 +	3.54		PTSRL
21 +	3.8		PTTRL
22 +	4.07		PTURL
23 +	5.96		PTVRL
24 +	5.62		PTWRL
25 +	5.78		PTXRL

EQUATION	111	IS	PTRLB
RHS +	0.0238		EQUAL

1 −	1.0	PTARL
2 −	1.0	PTBRL
3 −	1.0	PTCRL
4 −	1.0	PTDRL
5 −	1.0	PTERL
6 −	1.0	PTFRL
7 −	1.0	PTGRL
8 −	1.0	PTHRL
9 −	1.0	PTIRL
10 −	1.0	PTJRL
11 −	1.0	PTKRL
12 −	1.0	PTLRL
13 −	1.0	PTMRL
14 −	1.0	PTNRL
15 −	1.0	PTORL
16 −	1.0	PTPRL
17 −	1.0	PTQRL
18 +	1.0	PTRLB
19 −	1.0	PTRRL
20 −	1.0	PTSRL
21 −	1.0	PTTRL
22 −	1.0	PTURL
23 −	1.0	PTVRL
24 −	1.0	PTWRL
25 −	1.0	PTXRL

EQUATION	112	IS	PTVNB
RHS +	0.0		EQUAL

1 +	0.002917	PTNCB
2 −	1.0	PTVNB

EQUATION	113	IS	PTVTP
RHS +	0.0		EQUAL

1 +	0.001458	PTTAX
2 −	1.0	PTVTP

EQUATION	114	IS	SFDIS
RHS +	5.81		EQUAL

1 +	1.0	USDIS
2 +	1.0	UTDIS
3 +	1.0	WSDIS

EQUATION	115	IS	SVNCB
RHS +	0.0		EQUAL

1 +	1.0	SVBAL
2 −	1.0	SVNCB

EQUATION	116	IS	SVTAX
RHS +	0.1		LESS

1 +	1.0	4SVTAX

EQUATION	117	IS	TOARL
RHS +	0.0		EQUAL

1 +	1.0	2DARL
2 +	1.0	3BARL
3 +	1.0	CHARL
4 +	1.0	GFARL
5 +	1.0	PTARL
6 +	1.0	USARL

EQUATION	118	IS	TOBAL
RHS +	0.0		EQUAL

1 +	1.0	2DBAL
2 +	1.0	2YBAL
3 +	1.0	3BBAL
4 +	1.0	3SBAL
5 +	1.0	CHBAL
6 +	1.0	ESBAL
7 +	1.0	GFBAL
8 +	1.0	LSBAL
9 +	1.0	MNBAL
10 +	1.0	PTBAL
11 +	1.0	SVBAL
12 −	1.0	TOBAL
13 +	1.0	USBAL
14 +	1.0	UTBAL
15 +	1.0	WSBAL
16 +	1.0	WTBAL

EQUATION	119	IS	TOBRL
RHS +	0.0		EQUAL

1 +	1.0	2DBRL
2 +	1.0	3BBRL
3 +	1.0	CHBRL
4 +	1.0	GFBRL
5 +	1.0	PTBRL
6 +	1.0	USBRL

EQUATION	120	IS	TOCRL
RHS +	0.0		EQUAL

1 +	1.0	2DCRL
2 +	1.0	3BCRL
3 +	1.0	CHCRL
4 +	1.0	GFCRL
5 +	1.0	PTCRL
6 +	1.0	USCRL

EQUATION	121	IS	TODRL		EQUATION	126	IS	TOHRL
RHS +	0.0		EQUAL		RHS +	0.0		EQUAL
1 +	1.0		2DDRL		1 +	1.0		2DHRL
2 +	1.0		3BDRL		2 +	1.0		3BHRL
3 +	1.0		CHDRL		3 +	1.0		CHHRL
4 +	1.0		GFDRL		4 +	1.0		GFHRL
5 +	1.0		PTDRL		5 +	1.0		PTHRL
6 +	1.0		USDRL		6 +	1.0		USHRL
EQUATION	122	IS	TOERL		EQUATION	127	IS	TOIRL
RHS +	0.0		EQUAL		RHS +	0.0		EQUAL
1 +	1.0		2DERL		1 +	1.0		2DIRL
2 +	1.0		3BERL		2 +	1.0		3BIRL
3 +	1.0		CHERL		3 +	1.0		CHIRL
4 +	1.0		GFERL		4 +	1.0		GFIRL
5 +	1.0		PTERL		5 +	1.0		PTIRL
6 +	1.0		USERL		6 +	1.0		USIRL
EQUATION	123	IS	TOFEE		EQUATION	128	IS	TOJRL
RHS +	0.0		EQUAL		RHS +	0.0		EQUAL
1 +	1.0		CHFEE		1 +	1.0		2DJRL
2 +	1.0		GFFEE		2 +	1.0		3BJRL
3 +	1.0		PTFEE		3 +	1.0		CHJRL
4 −	1.0		TOFEE		4 +	1.0		GFJRL
5 +	1.0		USFEE		5 +	1.0		PTJRL
6 +	1.0		52DFEE		6 +	1.0		USJRL
EQUATION	124	IS	TOFRL		EQUATION	129	IS	TOKRL
RHS +	0.0		EQUAL		RHS +	0.0		EQUAL
1 +	1.0		2DFRL		1 +	1.0		2DKRL
2 +	1.0		3BFRL		2 +	1.0		3BKRL
3 +	1.0		CHFRL		3 +	1.0		CHKRL
4 +	1.0		GFFRL		4 +	1.0		GFKRL
5 +	1.0		PTFRL		5 +	1.0		PTKRL
6 +	1.0		USFRL		6 +	1.0		USKRL
EQUATION	125	IS	TOGRL		EQUATION	130	IS	TOLRL
RHS +	0.0		EQUAL		RHS +	0.0		EQUAL
1 +	1.0		2DGRL		1 +	1.0		2DLRL
2 +	1.0		3BGRL		2 +	1.0		3BLRL
3 +	1.0		CHGRL		3 +	1.0		CHLRL
4 +	1.0		GFGRL		4 +	1.0		GFLRL
5 +	1.0		PTGRL		5 +	1.0		PTLRL
6 +	1.0		USGRL		6 +	1.0		USLRL

EQUATION	131	IS	TOMRL
RHS +	0.0		EQUAL
1 +	1.0		2DMRL
2 +	1.0		3BMRL
3 +	1.0		CHMRL
4 +	1.0		GFMRL
5 +	1.0		PTMRL
6 +	1.0		USMRL

EQUATION	132	IS	TONRL
RHS +	0.0		EQUAL
1 +	1.0		2DNRL
2 +	1.0		3BNRL
3 +	1.0		CHNRL
4 +	1.0		GFNRL
5 +	1.0		PTNRL
6 +	1.0		USNRL

EQUATION	133	IS	TOORL
RHS +	0.0		EQUAL
1 +	1.0		2DORL
2 +	1.0		3BORL
3 +	1.0		CHORL
4 +	1.0		GFORL
5 +	1.0		PTORL
6 +	1.0		USORL

EQUATION	134	IS	TOPRL
RHS +	0.0		EQUAL
1 +	1.0		2DPRL
2 +	1.0		3BPRL
3 +	1.0		CHPRL
4 +	1.0		GFPRL
5 +	1.0		PTPRL
6 +	1.0		USPRL

EQUATION	135	IS	TOQRL
RHS +	0.0		EQUAL
1 +	1.0		2DQRL
2 +	1.0		3BQRL
3 +	1.0		CHQRL
4 +	1.0		GFQRL
5 +	1.0		PTQRL
6 +	1.0		USQRL

EQUATION	136	IS	TORCV
RHS −	0.494054		EQUAL
1 +	1.0		2DRCV
2 +	1.0		3BRCV
3 +	1.0		CHRCV
4 +	1.0		GFRCV
5 +	1.0		PTRCV
6 −	1.0		TORCV
7 +	1.0		USRCV

EQUATION	137	IS	TORRL
RHS +	0.0		EQUAL
1 +	1.0		2DRRL
2 +	1.0		3BRRL
3 +	1.0		CHRRL
4 +	1.0		GFRRL
5 +	1.0		PTRRL
6 +	1.0		USRRL

EQUATION	138	IS	TOSRL
RHS +	0.0		EQUAL
1 +	1.0		2DSRL
2 +	1.0		3BSRL
3 +	1.0		CHSRL
4 +	1.0		GFSRL
5 +	1.0		PTSRL
6 +	1.0		USSRL

EQUATION	139	IS	TOTAX
RHS +	4.003		EQUAL
1 +	1.0		3BTAX
2 +	1.0		CHTAX
3 +	1.0		HQTAX
4 +	1.0		LSTAX
5 +	1.0		PTTAX
6 +	1.0		USTAX
7 +	1.0		WTTAX
8 +	1.0		43STAX
9 +	1.0		4ESTAX
10 +	1.0		4SVTAX
11 +	1.0		4UTTAX
12 +	1.0		52DTAX

EQUATION	140	IS	TOTRL
RHS	+	0.0	EQUAL
1	+	1.0	2DTRL
2	+	1.0	3BTRL
3	+	1.0	CHTRL
4	+	1.0	GFTRL
5	+	1.0	PTTRL
6	+	1.0	USTRL

EQUATION	141	IS	TOURL
RHS	+	0.0	EQUAL
1	+	1.0	2DURL
2	+	1.0	3BURL
3	+	1.0	CHURL
4	+	1.0	GFURL
5	+	1.0	PTURL
6	+	1.0	USURL

EQUATION	142	IS	TOVRL
RHS	+	0.0	EQUAL
1	+	1.0	2DVRL
2	+	1.0	3BVRL
3	+	1.0	CHVRL
4	+	1.0	GFVRL
5	+	1.0	PTVRL
6	+	1.0	USVRL

EQUATION	143	IS	TOWRL
RHS	+	0.0	EQUAL
1	+	1.0	2DWRL
2	+	1.0	3BWRL
3	+	1.0	CHWRL
4	+	1.0	GFWRL
5	+	1.0	PTWRL
6	+	1.0	USWRL

EQUATION	144	IS	TOXRL
RHS	+	0.0	EQUAL
1	+	1.0	2DXRL
2	+	1.0	3BXRL
3	+	1.0	CHXRL
4	+	1.0	GFXRL
5	+	1.0	PTXRL
6	+	1.0	USXRL

EQUATION	145	IS	USCST
RHS	+	0.0	EQUAL
1	−	1.0	USCST
2	+	0.02	USCXD
3	+	0.05	USCXP
4	+	1.0	USMUC
5	−	1.0	USMUK
6	+	1.0	USOMC
7	+	0.034	USRLB
8	+	0.062	USWLB

EQUATION	146	IS	USCTN
RHS	+	0.0	EQUAL
1	−	2.77	USARL
2	−	2.7	USBRL
3	−	2.67	USCRL
4	+	1.0	USCTN
5	−	0.046685	USDEP
6	−	2.76	USDRL
7	−	2.56	USERL
8	−	2.75	USFRL
9	−	2.81	USGRL
10	−	2.83	USHRL
11	−	2.9	USIRL
12	−	2.63	USJRL
13	−	2.77	USKRL
14	−	2.46	USLRL
15	−	2.58	USMRL
16	−	2.46	USNRL
17	−	2.5	USORL
18	−	0.046685	USOTC
19	−	2.7	USPRL
20	−	2.9	USQRL
21	−	2.7	USRRL
22	−	2.82	USSRL
23	−	2.7	USTRL
24	−	2.9	USURL
25	−	2.74	USVRL
26	−	2.62	USWRL
27	−	0.046685	USWSD
28	−	1.69	USXRL

EQUATION	147	IS	USCXD
RHS	+	0.00065	EQUAL
1	+	1.0	USCXD

EQUATION	148	IS	USCXP
RHS +	0.0		EQUAL

1 +	1.0	USCXP
2 -	0.000818	USDIS

EQUATION	149	IS	USDEP
RHS +	4.82		EQUAL

1 +	1.0	USDEP

EQUATION	150	IS	USFEE
RHS +	0.0		GREATE

1 -	1.3	USCST
2 +	1.0	USFEE
3 +	1.3	USVNB
4 +	1.3	USVTP

EQUATION	151	IS	USMUC
RHS +	0.0		EQUAL

1 +	1.0	USMUC
2 -	1.0	USMUK

EQUATION	152	IS	USNCB
RHS +	0.0		EQUAL

1 +	1.0	USBAL
2 -	1.0	USCTN
3 +	0.26017	USDIS
4 -	1.0	USNCB
5 +	0.0775	USPAY

EQUATION	153	IS	USOMC
RHS +	0.000045		EQUAL

1 +	1.0	USOMC

EQUATION	154	IS	USOTC
RHS +	0.0		EQUAL

1 +	1.0	USOTC

EQUATION	155	IS	USPAY
RHS +	1.2		EQUAL

1 +	1.0	USPAY

EQUATION	156	IS	USRCV
RHS +	0.0		EQUAL

1 +	6.72	USARL
2 +	5.11	USBRL
3 +	5.21	USCRL
4 +	4.4	USDRL
5 +	5.27	USERL
6 +	5.4	USFRL
7 +	4.22	USGRL
8 +	4.35	USHRL
9 +	4.57	USIRL
10 +	4.07	USJRL
11 +	5.05	USKRL
12 +	4.49	USLRL
13 +	5.28	USMRL
14 +	5.17	USNRL
15 +	4.54	USORL
16 +	5.48	USPRL
17 +	4.2	USQRL
18 -	1.0	USRCV
19 +	4.2	USRRL
20 +	4.23	USSRL
21 +	3.14	USTRL
22 +	3.7	USURL
23 +	3.12	USVRL
24 +	2.68	USWRL
25 +	1.91	USXRL

EQUATION	157 IS	USRLB
RHS +	0.0551	EQUAL

1	−	1.0	USARL
2	−	1.0	USBRL
3	−	1.0	USCRL
4	−	1.0	USDRL
5	−	1.0	USERL
6	−	1.0	USFRL
7	−	1.0	USGRL
8	−	1.0	USHRL
9	−	1.0	USIRL
10	−	1.0	USJRL
11	−	1.0	USKRL
12	−	1.0	USLRL
13	−	1.0	USMRL
14	−	1.0	USNRL
15	−	1.0	USORL
16	−	1.0	USPRL
17	−	1.0	USQRL
18	+	1.0	USRLB
19	−	1.0	USRRL
20	−	1.0	USSRL
21	−	1.0	USTRL
22	−	1.0	USURL
23	−	1.0	USVRL
24	−	1.0	USWRL
25	−	1.0	USXRL

EQUATION	158 IS	USVNB
RHS +	0.0	EQUAL

1	+	0.002696	USNCB
2	−	1.0	USVNB

EQUATION	159 IS	USVTP
RHS +	0.0	EQUAL

1	+	0.001044	USTAX
2	−	1.0	USVTP

EQUATION	160 IS	USWLB
RHS +	0.00306	EQUAL

1	+	1.0	USWLB

EQUATION	161 IS	USWSD
RHS +	0.0	EQUAL

1	+	1.0	USWSD

EQUATION	162 IS	UTCST
RHS +	0.0	EQUAL

1	−	1.0	UTCST
2	+	0.04	UTCXP
3	+	1.0	UTMUC
4	−	1.0	UTMUK
5	+	1.0	UTOMC
6	+	0.065	UTWLB

EQUATION	163 IS	UTCTN
RHS +	0.0	EQUAL

1	+	1.0	UTCTN
2	−	0.053589	UTDEP

EQUATION	164 IS	UTCXP
RHS +	0.0	EQUAL

1	+	1.0	UTCXP
2	−	0.000818	UTDIS

EQUATION	165 IS	UTDEP
RHS +	3.44	EQUAL

1	+	1.0	UTDEP

EQUATION	166 IS	UTMUC
RHS +	0.0	EQUAL

1	+	1.0	UTMUC
2	−	1.0	UTMUK

EQUATION	167 IS	UTNCB
RHS +	0.0	EQUAL

1	+	1.0	UTBAL
2	−	1.0	UTCTN
3	+	0.2439	UTDIS
4	−	1.0	UTNCB

EQUATION	168 IS	UTOMC
RHS +	0.000055	EQUAL

1	+	1.0	UTOMC

EQUATION	169 IS	UTTAX
RHS +	0.3	LESS

1	+	1.0	4UTTAX

EQUATION	170	IS	UTVNB
RHS +	0.0		EQUAL
1 +	0.002262		UTNCB
2 -	1.0		UTVNB

EQUATION	171	IS	UTWLB
RHS +	0.00487		EQUAL
1 +	1.0		UTWLB

EQUATION	172	IS	WSCST
RHS +	0.0		EQUAL
1 -	1.0		WSCST
2 +	0.02		WSCXD
3 +	0.05		WSCXP
4 +	1.0		WSMUC
5 -	1.0		WSMUK
6 +	1.0		WSOMC

EQUATION	173	IS	WSCTN
RHS +	0.818		EQUAL
1 +	1.0		WSCTN

EQUATION	174	IS	WSCXD
RHS +	0.0031		EQUAL
1 +	1.0		WSCXD

EQUATION	175	IS	WSCXP
RHS +	0.0		EQUAL
1 +	1.0		WSCXP
2 -	0.00034		WSDIS
3 -	0.00034		WSHQD
4 -	0.002051		WSIDS

EQUATION	176	IS	WSHQD
RHS +	0.0		GREATE
1 -	0.2		NYHQD
2 +	1.0		WSHQD

EQUATION	177	IS	WSIDS
RHS +	0.39		EQUAL
1 +	1.0		WSIDS

EQUATION	178	IS	WSLNS
RHS +	5.8		EQUAL
1 +	1.0		WSLNS

EQUATION	179	IS	WSLNU
RHS +	7.0		EQUAL
1 +	1.0		WSLNU

EQUATION	180	IS	WSMUC
RHS +	0.0		EQUAL
1 +	1.0		WSMUC
2 -	1.0		WSMUK

EQUATION	181	IS	WSNCB
RHS +	0.0		EQUAL
1 +	1.0		WSBAL
2 -	1.0		WSCTN
3 +	0.25476		WSDIS
4 +	0.17807		WSHQD
5 +	0.38462		WSIDS
6 -	1.0		WSNCB

EQUATION	182	IS	WSOMC
RHS +	0.00006		EQUAL
1 +	1.0		WSOMC

EQUATION	183	IS	WSVNB
RHS +	0.0		EQUAL
1 +	0.003566		WSNCB
2 -	1.0		WSVNB

EQUATION	184	IS	WTCST
RHS +	0.0		EQUAL
1 -	1.0		WTCST
2 +	0.05		WTCXP
3 +	1.0		WTMUC
4 -	1.0		WTMUK
5 +	1.0		WTOMC
6 +	0.068		WTWLB

EQUATION	185	IS	WTCTN
RHS +	0.184		EQUAL
1 +	1.0		WTCTN

EQUATION	186	IS	WTCXP
RHS +	0.00346		EQUAL
1 +	1.0		WTCXP

```
EQUATION  187  IS  WTMUC          EQUATION  196  IS  12DVTP
RHS +     0.0      EQUAL          RHS +     0.0       LESS

  1 +     1.0      WTMUC            1 -     0.333333   2DTVL
  2 -     1.0      WTMUK            2 +     1.0        2DVTP

EQUATION  188  IS  WTNCB          EQUATION  197  IS  12YCST
RHS +     0.0      EQUAL          RHS +     0.0       LESS

  1 +     1.0      WTBAL            1 +     1.0        2YCST
  2 -     1.0      WTCTN            2 -     1.0        2YVNB
  3 -     1.0      WTNCB
  4 +     0.1203   WTPAY          EQUATION  198  IS  12YNCB
                                 RHS +     1.0       GREATE
EQUATION  189  IS  WTOMC
RHS +     0.00007  EQUAL            1 -     0.15       2YLNS
                                   2 -     0.1        2YLNU
  1 +     1.0      WTOMC            3 +     1.0        2YNCB

EQUATION  190  IS  WTPAY         EQUATION  199  IS  13BCST
RHS +     2.02     EQUAL          RHS +     0.0       LESS

  1 +     1.0      WTPAY            1 +     1.0        3BCST
                                   2 -     1.0        3BTVL
EQUATION  191  IS  WTTVL
RHS +     0.0      EQUAL          EQUATION  200  IS  13BNCB
                                 RHS +     0.5       GREATE
  1 -     1.0      WTTVL
  2 +     1.0      WTVNB            1 +     1.0        3BNCB
  3 +     1.0      WTVTP
                                 EQUATION  201  IS  13BVTP
EQUATION  192  IS  WTVNB         RHS +     0.0       LESS
RHS +     0.0      EQUAL
                                   1 -     0.333333   3BTVL
  1 +     0.002609 WTNCB            2 +     1.0        3BVTP
  2 -     1.0      WTVNB
                                 EQUATION  202  IS  13SNCB
EQUATION  193  IS  WTVTP         RHS +     0.25      GREATE
RHS +     0.0      EQUAL
                                   1 +     1.0        3SNCB
  1 +     0.001305 WTTAX            2 +     0.5        43STAX
  2 -     1.0      WTVTP
                                 EQUATION  203  IS  1CHCST
EQUATION  194  IS  WTWLB         RHS +     0.0       LESS
RHS +     0.00442  EQUAL
                                   1 +     1.0        CHCST
  1 +     1.0      WTWLB            2 -     1.0        CHTVL

EQUATION  195  IS  12DCST        EQUATION  204  IS  1CHNCB
RHS +     0.0      LESS          RHS +     0.5       GREATE

  1 +     1.0      2DCST            1 -     0.15       CHLNS
  2 -     1.0      2DTVL            2 +     1.0        CHNCB
```

EQUATION	205	IS	1CHVTP
RHS +	0.0		LESS

1 -	0.333333	CHTVL
2 +	1.0	CHVTP

EQUATION	206	IS	1ESNCB
RHS +	0.15		GREATE

1 +	1.0	ESNCB
2 +	0.5	4ESTAX

EQUATION	207	IS	1GFCST
RHS +	0.0		GREATE

1 -	1.0	GFCST
2 +	1.0	GFFEE
3 +	1.0	GFVNB

EQUATION	208	IS	1GFNCB
RHS +	0.0		GREATE

1 +	1.0	GFNCB

EQUATION	209	IS	1LSCST
RHS +	0.0		LESS

1 +	1.0	LSCST
2 -	1.0	LSTVL

EQUATION	210	IS	1LSNCB
RHS +	0.5		GREATE

1 -	0.15	LSLNS
2 +	1.0	LSNCB

EQUATION	211	IS	1MNCST
RHS +	0.0		LESS

1 +	1.0	MNCST
2 -	1.0	MNVNB

EQUATION	212	IS	1MNNCB
RHS +	1.0		GREATE

1 -	0.15	MNLNS
2 -	0.1	MNLNU
3 +	1.0	MNNCB

EQUATION	213	IS	1NYHQD
RHS +	14.65		EQUAL

1 +	1.0	NYHQD

EQUATION	214	IS	1PTCST
RHS +	0.0		GREATE

1 -	0.666667	PTCST
2 +	1.0	PTVNB
3 +	1.0	PTVTP

EQUATION	215	IS	1PTNCB
RHS +	0.0		GREATE

1 -	0.5	PTCTN
2 +	1.0	PTNCB

EQUATION	216	IS	1SVNCB
RHS +	0.1		GREATE

1 +	1.0	SVNCB
2 +	0.5	4SVTAX

EQUATION	217	IS	1USNCB
RHS +	0.5		GREATE

1 +	1.0	USNCB

EQUATION	218	IS	1USVTP
RHS +	0.0		LESS

1 -	0.333333	USCST
2 +	1.0	USVTP

EQUATION	219	IS	1UTCST
RHS +	0.0		LESS

1 +	1.0	UTCST
2 -	1.0	UTVNB

EQUATION	220	IS	1UTNCB
RHS +	0.35		GREATE

1 +	1.0	UTNCB
2 +	0.5	4UTTAX

EQUATION	221	IS	1WSCST
RHS +	0.0		LESS

1 +	1.0	WSCST
2 -	1.0	WSVNB

EQUATION	222	IS	1WSNCB
RHS +	1.0		GREATE

1 -	0.15	WSLNS
2 -	0.1	WSLNU
3 +	1.0	WSNCB

EQUATION	223	IS	1WTCST
RHS +	0.0		LESS

1 +	1.0	WTCST
2 –	1.0	WTTVL

EQUATION	224	IS	1WTNCB
RHS +	0.0		GREATE

1 –	0.5	WTCTN
2 +	1.0	WTNCB

EQUATION	225	IS	1WTVTP
RHS +	0.0		LESS

1 –	0.5	WTTVL
2 +	1.0	WTVTP

EQUATION	226	IS	22YNCB
RHS +	3.1		GREATE

1 +	1.0	2YNCB

EQUATION	227	IS	2WSNCB
RHS +	4.0		GREATE

1 +	1.0	WSNCB

EQUATION	228	IS	52DACT
RHS +	0.0		EQUAL

1 –	1.0	52DACT
2 +	1.0	52DCXP
3 +	1.0	52DFEE
4 +	1.0	52DNCB
5 +	1.0	52DOMC
6 +	1.0	52DRLB
7 +	1.0	52DTAX

EQUATION	229	IS	52DOMC
RHS +	0.00009		GREATE

1 +	1.0	2DOMC

CASH ALPHA Solution - Base Case
Optimal Solution

J(H)	BETA(H)	RCW(I)	PI'(I)
0 CCOCO	.1241536S-	CCC	1.CCCCOCOC
C CCOOO	.1241536S-	CC1	.
0 CCOCC	.1241536S-	CC2	.
C CCOOC	7.4304CEES	C1C	.
2CCST	.CC217C88	2CCST	6.C305EC42
2CCTN	.1C48C264	2DCTN	.C151C655-
2CCXP	.0022225S	2CCXP	.36183363-
2CDEP	1.76900000	2CDEP	.CCC8S4S7-
2CDIS	4.2SS64779	+ 2CFEE	.
2CMUC	.	2CMUC	6.C305EC42-
2CNCB	.86661679	2CNCB	.C151C655-
2COMC	.000125CC	2COMC	6.C3056C42-
2CRLB	.C4250C0C	2DRCV	.C6319374-
2CTVL	.CC217088	2DRLE	.27137522-
2CVNB	.CC217088	2DTVL	6.C3056C42-
2CVRL	.	2DVNB	6.C3C56C42-
2YCST	.CCC9SC98	2CVTP	4926.11329251-
2YCTN	.	2YCST	.
2YCXP	.CC841961	2YCTN	.C1566454-
2YDIS	3.5387C9CS	2YCXP	.
2YDIV	.75CCCCCC	2YDIV	.CC356835
2YDXP	.C112C000	2YDXP	.
2YHCD	10.255CCCCC	- 2YHQD	.
2YLNS	7.10CCCCCC	2YLNS	.
2YLNU	5.CCCCCCCC	2YLNU	.
2YMUC	.	2YMUC	.
2YNCB	3.1CCCCCCC	2YNCB	.C1566454-
2YOMC	.CCCC1CCC	2YOMC	.
2YVNB	.C11C546C	2YVNB	.
3BARL	.	3BCST	.C1C9C511
3EBAL	.5623C1S1	3BCTN	.C1666700-
3BCST	.0011SS2C	3BCXD	.CC032715-
3BCTN	.C623C1S1	3BCXP	.C137815C
3BCXC	.001540CC	3BDEP	.CCC54796-
3BDEP	1.E9SCCCCC	3BMUC	.C1C9C511-
3BDIS	.	3BNCB	.C1666700-
3BFRL	.	3BCMC	.C1C9C511-
3BMUC	.	3BCTC	.00054796-
3BNCB	.5CCCCCCC	3BRCV	.CCCS1186-
3BOMC	.CCC14500	3BRLB	.CC032715-
3BOTC	.	3BTVL	.C1C9C511-
3BRLB	.C336C0CC	3BVNB	.C1C9C511-
3BTAX	.39880C43	3BVTP	.C1C90511-
3BTRL	.	3SNCB	.C1666700-
3BTVL	.CC11SS2C	+ 3STAX	.
3BVNB	.0C08235C	BADIS	.CC306889
3BVRL	.	CADIS	.CC322596

Optimal Solution Value		Marginal Cost	
3BVIP	.CCC3657C	CHCST	.6683C9C3
3SBAL	.25C0CCCC	CHCTN	.C1666700-
3SNCB	.25CCCCCC	CHCXC	.C1336618-
CHBAL	.81375139	CHCXP	.C3341545-
CHCST	.CC31E75E	CHDEP	.CCC84385-
CHCTN	.37101664 +	CHFEE	•
CHCXC	.CCC7CCCC	CHLNS	.CC196515-
CHCXP	.C0C29163	CHMUC	.6683C9C3-
CHDEP	7.3280CCCC	CHNCB	.C1666700-
CHDIS	.56408474	CHCMC	.6683C9C3-
CHFEE	.CCC15484	CHCTC	.CCC843E5-
CHGRL	•	CHRCV	.CC613136-
CHLNS	.35CCCCCC	CHRLB	.C25C6159-
CHMUK	•	CHTVL	1.CCCOCCCC-
CHNCE	.5525CCCC	CHVNB	1.CCCCCCCC-
CHCMC	.CCCCSOCC	CHVTP	.CC4S261C-
CHDTC	•	CHWLB	.C4344CCS-
CHRLB	.C73CCCCC	CHWSD	.CCC84385-
CHTAX	.5234118S	ESNCB	.C1666700-
CHTVL	.CC31E75E	ESTAX	•
CHVNB	.CC197C21	GFCST	1.0CCCCCCC
CHVRL	•	GFCTN	.CCCCC412-
CHVTP	.CC1C6253	GFCXP	.C5CCCCCC-
CHWLB	.CC51CCCC +	GFDIS	•
CHWSC	•	GFMUC	1.CCCCCCCC-
ESBAL	.15COCCCC	GFNCB	.CC25CCCC-
ESNCB	.15CCCCCC	GFOMC	1.CCCCCCCC-
GFCST	•	GFRCV	.CCCC04592-
GFCXP	•	GFRLB	.C425CCCC-
GFFEE	•	GFVNB	1.CCCCCCCC-
GFMUK	•	LSCST	•
GFNCB	•	LSCTN	.C1583136-
GFOMC	•	LSCXP	•
GFQRL	•	LSDEP	.CCCSCC44-
GFRLB	•	LSLNS	.CC23747C-
GFSRL	•	LSMUC	•
GFURL	•	LSNCB	.C1583136-
GFVNB	•	LSCMC	•
GFVRL	•	LSPAY	.CC24C39S
GFWRL	•	LSTVL	•
GFXRL	•	LSVNB	•
HGTAX	1.578727C1	LSVTP	•
LSCST	.CC051667	LSWLB	•
LSCTN	.34751847	MNCST	•
C CCOCO	•	MNCTN	•
LSCXP	.CCC61914	MNCXP	•
LSDEP	6.11CCCCCC	− MNGC	.CCC02712-
LSDIS	1.19755837	MNLNS	.CC25CCC5-

148

Optimal Solution Value		Marginal Cost	
LSLNS	.35CCCCCC	MNLNU	.CC16667C-
LSMUC	.	MNMUC	.
LSNCB	.5525CCCC	MNNCB	.C16667CC-
LSGMC	.CCC1CCCC	MNCMC	.
LSPAY	4.32CCCCCC	MNVNB	.
LSTVL	.CCC96135	NGTAX	.CCE32350
LSVNB	.CCC96135	NYHGD	.CC333185
LSVTP	.	PTCST	.CC685870
LSWLB	.CC79CCCC	PTCTN	.C243C47S-
MNBAL	1.15581416	PTCXP	.CCC34254-
MNCST	.CC2C6CS4	PTDEP	.CC133C44-
MNCXP	.CCC55E8S	− PTFEE	.CC54E6S6-
MNDIS	1.4725C3C5	PTMUC	.CC685870
MNHGC	1.465CCCCC	PTNCB	.C162CS86-
MNLNS	3.C5CCCCCC	PTCMC	.CC685870-
MNLNU	3.CCCCCCCC	PTRCV	.CC47E6C4-
MNMUC	.	PTRLB	.CCC24CC5-
MNNCB	1.7575CCCC	FTVNB	.CC685870-
MNOMC	.CC2C11CC	FTVTP	.CC685870-
MNVNB	.CC626724	SFDIS	.CC4246CE
NYHGD	14.65CCCCCC	SVNCB	.C16667CC-
PTCRL	.	+ SVTAX	.
PTCST	.CCCS2S5C	TCARL	.02175263-
PTCTN	.C5265S88	TCBAL	.C16667CC
PTCXP	.CC112SS2	TCBRL	.03335653-
PTDEP	.562CCCCC	TCCRL	.C3C42856-
PTDIS	.4170S6S5	TCDRL	.C4CC2687-
PTMUC	.	TCERL	.C2S82C88-
PTNCB	.C2632SS4	TCFEE	1.CCCCCCCC
PTCMC	.CCCC4CCC	TCFRL	.C2C85295-
PTRLB	.C238CCCC	TCGRL	.C4154152-
PTTAX	.58483632	TCHRL	.C4157626-
PTVNB	.CCCC768C	TCIRL	.C4C97S76-
PTVRL	.	TCJRL	.C4C51C20-
PTVTP	.CC085269	TCKRL	.C35C254C-
SVBAL	.1CCCCCCC	TCLRL	.C3437442-
SVNCB	.1CCCCCCC	TCMRL	.C3CC7C55-
TCBAL	6.S3635469	TCNRL	.C2ES6SS4-
TCFEE	.CCC32685	TCCRL	.C3463532-
TCRCV	.454054CC	TCPRL	.C3C45586-
USARL	.	TCQRL	.C4232548-
USBRL	.	TCRCV	.C16667CC
USCST	.CC222C48	TCRRL	.C4C62895-
USCTN	.2250217C	TCSRL	.C4236542-
USCXC	.CCC65CCC	TCTAX	.CCCC1CCC
USCXP	.CC198714	TCTRL	.C4C54C7S-
USDEP	4.82CCCCCC	TCURL	.C4227818-
USDIS	2.42926433	TCVRL	.C4218725-

Optimal Solution Value		Marginal Cost	
USDRL	.	TChRL	.C422C596-
USERL	.	TCXRL	.C422C763-
USFEE	.CCC172C1	USCST	.86985994
USHRL	.	LSCTN	.C1645717-
USIRL	.	LSCXD	.C173972C-
USJRL	.	LSCXP	.C43493CC-
USKRL	.	LSDEP	.CCC7683C-
USLRL	.	LSFEE	1.CCCCCCCC-
USMRL	.	LSMUC	.86985994-
USMUK	.	LSNCB	.C1645717-
USNCB	.5CCCCCCC	LSCMC	.86985994-
USNRL	.	LSCTC	.CCC7683C-
LSOMC	.CCCC45CC	LSPAY	.CC127543
LSORL	.	LSRCV	.CC79477E-
LSOTC	.	LSRLB	.C2957524-
LSPAY	1.2CCCCCCC	LSVNB	1.3CCCCCCC-
USPRL	.	LSVTP	.CC957853-
USRLB	.C551CCCC	LSWLB	.C5393132-
LSRRL	.	LSWSD	.CCC7683C-
USSRL	.	UTCST	.
LSTAX	.7CE9638Z	UTCTN	.C1666700-
USVNB	.CC1348CC	LTCXP	.22127582
LSVTP	.CCC74C16	UTDEP	.CCC89317-
USWLB	.CC3C6CCC	UTMUC	.
LSWSD	.	UTNCB	.C1666700-
USXRL	.	UTCMC	.
UTBAL	.5343461E	+ UTTAX	.
LTCST	.CCC37155	UTVNB	.
UTCTN	.1843461E	UTWLB	.
UTDEP	3.44CCCCC	WSCST	.
UTDIS	.	WSCTN	.C1666700-
UTMUC	.	WSCXD	.
UTNCB	.35CCCCCC	WSCXP	.
UTCMC	.CCCC55CC	- WSHCD	.CCC3639E-
UTVNB	.CCC7917C	WSICS	.CC641C46
UTWLB	.CC487CCC	WSLNS	.
WSBAL	3.2849768E	WSLNU	.
WSCST	.CCC2692E	WSMUC	.
WSCTN	.818CCCCC	WSNCB	.C1666700-
WSCXD	.CC31CCCC	WSCMC	.
WSCXP	.CC294554	WSVNB	.
WSDIS	3.38C73567	WTCST	3.19796711
WSHCD	2.93CCCCCC	WTCTN	.C1666700-
WSICS	.39CCCCCC	WTCXP	.15989E3E-
WSLNS	5.6CCCCCCC	WTMUC	3.19796711-
WSLNU	7.CCCCCCCC	WTNCE	.C1666700-
WSMUC	.	WTCMC	3.19796711-
WSNCB	4.CCCCCCCC	WTPAY	.CC2CC5C4

Optimal Solution Value		Marginal Cost	
hSCMC	.CCCC6CCC	hTTVL	6.3EE27139-
hSVNB	.C14264CC	hTVNB	6.3EE27139-
hTBAL	.C451641E	hTVTP	.CC766283-
hTCST	.CCC54356	hTWLB	.21746176-
hTCTN	.184CCCCC	+12DCST	6.C3C56C42
hTCXP	.CC346CCC	+12CVTP	•
hTMLK	•	+12YCST	•
hTNCB	.1C417C1E	-12YNCB	•
hTOMC	.CCCC7CCC	+13BCST	.C1C9C511
hTPAY	2.C2CCCCCC	-13BNCB	.C1664882-
hTTAX	.2C826C54	+13BVTP	•
hTTVL	.CCC54356	-13SNCB	.C16667CC-
hTVNB	.CCC2717E	+1CHCST	.6683C9C3
hTVTP	.CCC2717E	-1CHNCB	.C131C1CC-
hTWLB	.CC442CCC	+1CHVTP	.S95C739C
4LTTAX	•	-1ESNCB	.C16667CC-
52CACT	•	-1GFCST	1.CCCCCCCC-
52CTAX	•	-1GFNCB	•
+ 2CFEE	.CCC72362	+1LSCST	•
- 2YHGC	7.325CCCCC	-1LSNCB	.C158313E-
+ 3STAX	.2CCCCCCC	+1MNCST	•
+ CHFEE	.CCC9C7E9	-1MNNCB	.C16667CC-
+ ESTAX	.1CCCCCCC	1NYHQD	.CC325635
+ GFDIS	•	-1PTCST	•
+ SVTAX	.1CCCCCCC	-1PTNCB	.C1E18SE6-
+ LTTAX	.3CCCCCCC	-1SVNCB	.C16667CC-
+12CVTP	.CCC72362	-1USNCB	.C1295237-
+12YCST	.C1CC6362	+1LSVTP	1.29C42147
-12YNCB	.535CCCCC	+1LTCST	•
+13BVTP	.CCCC34C3	-1LTNCB	.C16667CC-
-1GFNCB	•	+1hSCST	•
+1LSCST	.CCC44468	-1hSNCB	•
+1MNCST	.CC42C63C	+1hTCST	3.19796711
-1PTCST	.CCC3C9E3	-1hTNCE	•
+1UTCST	.CCC42C15	+1hTVTP	6.3EC6CE57
+1hSCST	.C1399472	-22YNCB	.C1566454-
-1hSNCB	1.43CCCCCC	-2hSNCB	.C16667CC-
-1hTNCB	.C1217C1E	52CACT	1C.CCCCCCCC
-52CCMC	.CCCC35CC	-52CCMC	•

CASH ALPHA Solution - Base Case
Delta j's

(Note: This is a summary of the relevant delta-j's from the solution print-out.)

2DBAL	.00156045
2YBAL	.00100246
3BCXP	.01432675
LSTAX	.00001000
PTBAL	.00045714
PTFEE	.99451304
USBAL	.00020983
UTCXP	.22127582

INDEX